More Praise for *Execution IS the Strategy*

"*Execution IS the Strategy* is a powerful formula to crack the code and turn the table on strategic planning."
—**Alan J. Maxwell, Head of Global HR Transformation, Lockheed Martin**

"I'm glad to see that even as Laura Stack emphasizes her key message of execution and results, she continuously brings readers back to the importance of people—teamwork, collaboration, empowerment, trust. Why? Because she knows that without your people, you're nothing."
—**Ken Blanchard, coauthor of *The One Minute Manager* and *Trust Works!***

"Borrow from Laura Stack's twenty-two years of execution excellence to create your culture of high performance and *big results*."
—**Darren Hardy, Publisher and Founding Editor, *Success* magazine, and *New York Times* bestselling author of *The Compound Effect***

"Laura Stack's great book addresses every leader's unique execution challenges!"
—**Jennifer Colosimo, Vice President of Wisdom, DaVita Healthcare Partners, and coauthor of *Great Work, Great Career* (with Stephen R. Covey)**

"*Execution IS the Strategy* is the handbook for leaders to diagnose and execute with exceptional results. I recommend this book to all leaders who want to develop the ability to turn at the speed of now."
—**Jeff Bettinger, Director, Leadership and Organizational Development, Petco**

"A fresh take from Laura Stack on how to blow up obstacles to efficient execution. If you want your employees and teams to be more productive, read this book!"
—**Randy Gage, author of the *New York Times* bestseller *Risky Is the New Safe***

"Innovation doesn't happen until the idea makes its way to the market through flawless execution. Laura Stack captures this truism, and adds to the discussion with a blueprint on how to finish excellent ideas well. Buy a copy for every manager at your company and your CFO will thank you later!"
—**Tim Sanders, author of *Love Is the Killer App: How to Win Business and Influence Friends***

"This book is chock-full of helpful ideas to assist leaders in ongoing efforts to get things done more effectively. I encourage you to take two major steps toward enhanced execution today—first buy, then read *Execution IS the Strategy*."

—**Phillip Van Hooser, speaker, trainer, and author of *Leaders Ought to Know***

"Laura's all about saving time, and she makes a convincing case that long-term strategic plans don't work well with today's business conditions. Read *Execution IS the Strategy*, and you'll learn how to seize opportunities, act on ideas, and be ready for anything."

—**Laura Vanderkam, author of *What the Most Successful People Do before Breakfast***

"Laura Stack not only inspires action but gives us incredibly practical guidelines for the effective execution of ideas that will drive positive results."

—**Joe Calloway, author of *Be the Best at What Matters Most***

"This book encourages you to re-evaluate your way of thinking to achieve goals in an efficient and effective manner. Maximize your execution efforts through these proven strategies!"

—**Dr. Nido Qubein, President, High Point University, and Chairman, Great Harvest Bread Co.**

"Laura Stack's newest book elevates her concepts to the leadership level and shows you how to empower your team members to efficiently execute your strategic priorities. Don't just read this book—execute the ideas inside this book. You will be glad you did!"

—**Shep Hyken, *New York Times* and *Wall Street Journal* bestselling author of *The Amazement Revolution***

"*Execution IS the Strategy* shows leaders how to shift strategic course quickly and turn on a dime. Learn to lean on your team members and make solid, reliable decisions to best execute your priorities and get things done."

—**Eric Chester, author of *On Fire at Work***

"Laura Stack's approaches to maximizing your productivity are tangible and easy to implement. Anything she writes is a must-read!"

—**Laurie McDonald, Director, Sales Effectiveness, Kronos Incorporated**

"Laura Stack shows you how to throw out the strategies of old and get focused on the things that will drive your business forward."

—Rory Vaden, cofounder of Southwestern Consulting and *New York Times* bestselling author of *Take the Stairs*

"This powerful, practical book gives you a set of proven tools to equip your leaders with the knowledge, skills, and inspiration to turn your strategy into performance. When you apply these simple principles, your employees and teams can start getting more done, faster, than ever before."

—Brian Tracy, author of *No Excuses!*

"The #1 Productivity Pro offers practical and effective tips to ensure competitive success. Her book is a road map to gain the best outcomes. I wouldn't want to navigate without it."

—Tim Jackson, CMP, CAE, President/CEO, Colorado Automobile Dealers Association

"After reading *Execution IS the Strategy*, you'll have all the tools and techniques you need to execute your ideas quickly and benefit from the results. The only question is, what are you waiting for?"

—Bruce Turkel, CEO/Executive Creative Director, Turkel Brands

"*Execution IS the Strategy* is a must-read for leaders who want to learn how to create agile organizational cultures that can drive initiatives forward."

—Daniel Burrus, author of the *New York Times* bestseller *Flash Foresight*

"Laura Stack has demystified strategy to be accessible, actionable, urgent, and even fun. She shows us how to apply it to work and life and understand that it is ultimately about taking action despite uncertainty."

—G. Shawn Hunter, author of *Out Think*

"Laura Stack goes beyond the to-do list and good intentions to a strategic approach for execution. If you follow her advice, you will have no excuses not to move forward on needed changes, and it will make you a more successful leader."

—Lisa Ford, author and speaker on helping companies create customer-focused cultures

"*Execution IS the Strategy* is packed full of relevant, real-world, actionable tactics that will elevate your performance as a leader and deliver results that count."

—Lt. Col. Rob "Waldo" Waldman, author of the *New York Times* and *Wall Street Journal* bestseller *Never Fly Solo*

"Laura Stack does a masterful job of weaving together elements of leadership, program, change, and her famous time management techniques in a simple, easy-to-implement format. She is my shortcut to excellence."

—Eva J. Milko, Senior Director, Global Procurement, Molson Coors Brewing Company, and author of *10 Steps to Effective Execution in Strategic Sourcing*

"*Execution IS the Strategy* is a must-read for leaders in any industry. This step-by-step guide can help you manufacture the one thing you need the most—time!"

—Anthony DiBlasi, Director, Merrill Lynch

"*Execution IS the Strategy* puts the final nail in the coffin of micromanaging, overplanning, and control-freakism. Simply put, it's brilliant. Do yourself, your team, and your organization a favor—buy it, download it, and share it. I have, and the results are amazing."

—Simon T. Bailey, leadership catalyst and author of *Release Your Brilliance*

"Laura Stack provides practical, easy-to-implement techniques to ensure your team is equipped to properly execute your core business objectives with precision and speed. Highly recommended."

—Matt Schupp, Vice President of Human Resources, The Sherwin-Williams Company, Southeastern Division

"Laura Stack's new book is easy to understand, remember, and implement. There is always something to learn on every page—including the table of contents!"

—Hervé Borensztejn, Managing Partner, Karistem Corporate Consulting, speaker, trainer, and editor of *Growing Talent*

"Laura Stack provides a simple yet powerful blueprint for bringing ideas to fruition. Anyone in a leadership position who does not read *Execution IS the Strategy* should be immediately executed!"

—Stephen Shapiro, innovation evangelist and author of *Best Practices Are Stupid*

EXECUTION
IS THE STRATEGY

OTHER BOOKS BY LAURA STACK

What to Do When There's Too Much to Do
Reduce Tasks, Increase Results, and Save 90 Minutes a Day

SuperCompetent
The Six Keys to Perform at Your Productive Best

The Exhaustion Cure
Up Your Energy from Low to Go in 21 Days

Find More Time
How to Get Things Done at Home, Organize Your Life,
and Feel Great About It

Leave the Office Earlier
How to Do More in Less Time and Feel Great About It

EXECUTION **IS** THE STRATEGY

How Leaders Achieve
Maximum Results
in **Minimum Time**

Laura Stack

BK

Berrett–Koehler Publishers, Inc.
San Francisco
a BK Business book

Berrett-Koehler Publishers, Inc.
235 Montgomery Street, Suite 650
San Francisco, CA 94104-2916
Tel: (415) 288-0260   Fax: (415) 362-2512   www.bkconnection.com

Ordering Information

Quantity sales. Special discounts are available on quantity purchases by corporations, associations, and others. For details, contact the "Special Sales Department" at the Berrett-Koehler address above.

Individual sales. Berrett-Koehler publications are available through most bookstores. They can also be ordered directly from Berrett-Koehler: Tel: (800) 929-2929; Fax: (802) 864-7626; www.bkconnection.com

Orders for college textbook/course adoption use. Please contact Berrett-Koehler: Tel: (800) 929-2929; Fax: (802) 864-7626.

Orders by U.S. trade bookstores and wholesalers. Please contact Ingram Publisher Services, Tel: (800) 509-4887; Fax: (800) 838-1149; E-mail: customer .service@ingrampublisherservices.com; or visit www.ingrampublisherservices .com/Ordering for details about electronic ordering.

Berrett-Koehler and the BK logo are registered trademarks of Berrett-Koehler Publishers, Inc.

Printed in the United States of America

Berrett-Koehler books are printed on long-lasting acid-free paper. When it is available, we choose paper that has been manufactured by environmentally responsible processes. These may include using trees grown in sustainable forests, incorporating recycled paper, minimizing chlorine in bleaching, or recycling the energy produced at the paper mill.

Library of Congress Cataloging-in-Publication Data
Stack, Laura.
    Execution is the strategy : how leaders achieve maximum results in minimum time / Laura Stack.
        pages cm
    Includes bibliographical references and index.
    ISBN 978-1-60994-968-6 (pbk.)
1. Strategic planning.   2. Organizational effectiveness.   3. Leadership.
I. Title.
    HD30.28.S665 2014
    658.4'012—dc23   2013047299

First Edition

18 17 16 15 14   10 9 8 7 6 5 4 3 2 1

Produced by Wilsted & Taylor Publishing Services

Project manager Christine Taylor   *Copy editor* Nancy Evans
Designer Nancy Koerner   *Indexer* Andrew Joron

Cover design: Daniel Tesser/pemastudio

› To Dianna Booher

A second mom, a sister,
a dear friend, and a mentor
wrapped up in one.

Thank you for your inspiration
to keep writing, your words
of encouragement, and your
never-ending love and support.

Contents

EXECUTION
IS THE STRATEGY

Strategic Planning Is So Yesterday, But Execution Is Always in Style

You did your off-site strategy session, enjoyed the golf outing, and then took off on vacation. You're feeling well-rested, glowing with a sense of accomplishment. But it's been four weeks, and you still haven't briefed your directors and managers on your stellar strategy. So what do you actually have? *No* strategy. It's a nice thought; it looks good; you crossed it off your list. But here's the reality: You are General Custer, and five thousand Indian ponies are bearing down on you from all directions. Your troops don't know what to do. Dust fills their eyes—and yours.

If you want to avoid a massacre, don't put down this book. In it, you'll learn how to arm your troops more effectively and execute strategy on the front lines—because you can't fire their guns for them.

THE FOUR PREMISES OF STRATEGY

Like the old gray mare of legend, strategic execution just ain't what it used to be—a point that hit home repeatedly as I conducted interviews with high-level executives in a number of industries.

1

John Alberto, Senior Vice President of Human Resources at Combe, Inc., started our interview with this warning: "I'll begin by telling you my bias on strategic plans: they're a waste of time. You prepare a strategic plan and then put it on the shelf, while the real world passes you by. When you pull it out, everybody says, 'We didn't do any of that.'"

You may recognize Combe as the manufacturer of personal care products like Just for Men, Sea-Bond, Brylcreem, and Aqua Velva. Alberto said,

> In the 1990s, we used to do five-year strategic plans all the way down to fairly detailed financial numbers. These would include a whole host of things related to the brands, the marketing of the brands, where we would go around the world with different brands, plus a five-year view of new products.
>
> Frankly, if after a year or two the plan still had some validity, it would be surprising. Later, we shortened it to three-year strategic plans with less detailed financials. Then a funny thing happened, at least in the consumer products industry: the lifespan of a chief marketing officer became about eighteen months. The lifespan of CEOs tends to be about three years, so a three-year strategic plan didn't work either.

Ideally, a strategic plan serves as a vehicle for continually reminding executives and other organizational leaders to evaluate the direction of their businesses according to their overall goals. But, as Alberto can attest, this doesn't always happen. Why? Because there's barely enough time to stop and take a breath anymore—much less implement a tool that may be stale before it's a month old.

Today leaders lean on their team members—the troops on the front lines—to help them make solid, reliable decisions on how to best execute the objectives that advance the ultimate organizational strategy; hence the title of this book: *Execution IS the Strategy*. This strategy builds on four basic premises that I call interdependency, fluidity, speed, and validity.

I doubt anyone reading this book will disagree with these premises, because you've observed the truths in your business. Let's take a closer look at them and see how they affect strategic execution.

THE FOUR PREMISES OF STRATEGY

1 *Interdependency.* Strategy and tactics are part of the same over-arching process, with an inherent relationship.

2 *Fluidity.* Strategy must be more flexible in its tactics now than in the past.

3 *Speed.* Strategy must be executed more quickly than ever before to be effective.

4 *Validity.* Strategy must still be appropriate and strong, or none of the first three premises matters.

Interdependency

Understanding how goals, strategies, and tactics interrelate can be confusing, so let's lay out some operational definitions.

A *goal* is something you want to accomplish within a specific time frame (sometimes interchangeably called a strategic objective or a strategic priority). *Strategy* is your long-term plan or alternative methods of accomplishing that goal. *Tactics* are the short-term actions required to fulfill a selected strategy. *Execution* is the process of moving from the statement of a goal to the completion of a tactic. In its most simplistic sense, I define execution as moving from a goal to a check mark. Efficient execution is the shortest distance between a goal and a check mark. Effective execution, then, is the most profitable outcome of the distance between a goal and a check mark. Efficiency and effectiveness aren't always the same thing, as you know. In this book, you'll note my bias toward efficiency, and in most cases I'll assume you have an effective strategy. I am not a strategist; I am an efficiency expert.

Let's say your goal is to get to your office safely and quickly. One strategy may be to "avoid traffic jams." Potential tactics for accomplishing this strategy may include biking to work, leaving early to avoid traffic, checking the traffic on your GPS before setting out, taking the back streets, riding the bus, or hopping on the subway or light rail. Depending on the intersection of these tactics and a variety of other factors (road conditions, weather, distance, convenience, hassle, etc.), your tactics may vary daily.

A carpool might allow you to work during the commute (an efficient use of time), but you're limited in your flexibility to leave early (and therefore not very effective). If you plan to head to the Great American Beer Festival in downtown Denver after work and enjoy a few beers while there, you may decide taking the light rail to and from downtown that day will be the best way to accomplish your goal. In addition, deciding a month in advance that you'll take the local E-470 bypass to the airport won't work if you wake up that day and find it under construction. You'll need to implement an alternate tactic to execute your strategy in the moment. In other words, tactics can vary daily and, in fact, by the minute. This variation is the essential problem of trying to plan a strategy further ahead than a few months, because our environment changes so quickly.

During my tenure on the board of the National Speakers Association (I was the 2011–2012 NSA President), I participated in many "strategic planning" sessions. NSA board members would determine where the association should be in three years and give the staff its marching orders, all the way down to the tactical "to-do" plan. We would really get into the weeds with all the detail. The following year, NSA staff members reported what they actually did, which wasn't what we board members (in our infinite wisdom) had dictated. The staff reacted to opportunities that often weren't in the plan. They were the ones with their feet on the street and their ears to the ground, so this was perfectly appropriate. Telling them what to do from afar wasn't the best strategy. We were paying them to think.

Perhaps in your organization, once upon a time, leadership considered strategy and operations to be separate functions, just as we did. Sometimes leadership still does. Senior executives conducted "Strategy" with outside consultants during week-long, cabin-in-the-woods retreats, and "Operations" was the downstream piece. The leaders would decide what to do going forward, and the troops would carry out their wishes.

Alberto explained Combe's current process this way:

Today, the executive team meets to put together broad financial goals. We do a SWOT analysis—the strengths, weaknesses, opportunities, threats—and then we take it down to our key categories. We look at gaps, and then, from those gaps, we come up with our strategic priorities. The process ends up taking fewer than two days. Most senior execs have been in the business a while, so they get it. The gaps are quite obvious.

The question then becomes, "How do we execute against the gaps?" Before, we'd go away for a week and sit around doing a lot of talking. We'd have a leader—sometimes an outside person—take us through the process. Now, it's much shorter and much quicker. Things revolve around growth at the top-line level, which then flows through all the way to the bottom line. We have checkpoints about three times a year, which take around two hours.

When an organization sees an opportunity or realizes a threat, it can't apply the same old change process that worked years ago. That process is no longer capable of winning in today's fast-paced business environment. By the time you've written your strategic plan and the printer has cooled down, it's already out of date. Goals, strategy, tactics, and execution should be part of the same dynamic process—implementing long-term priorities through short-term, daily operations.

Fluidity

As a leader, it's important to articulate the organization's strategy clearly—indeed, you must be specific in your definition of what constitutes "success." That said, the strategy itself must be extremely fluid in its tactics, so that the frontline workers are encouraged to determine how best to achieve it. You'll realize better results if you create an agile culture full of flexible, strategic thinkers who remain focused on the overall goals and the roles they play in achieving them. They must be willing to both entertain and implement new tactics for doing so, even with minimal warning.

In today's business world, leaders usher in change by fostering risk-taking and creativity. Operations adjust to achieve strategic priorities dynamically, often creating the future in the moment. Company leaders lick a finger and stick it in the air to determine where the winds of change are blowing. From there, they quickly shift direction to catch the breeze and fill the sails. In an effective change process, leaders communicate the organization's strategic priorities directly to all team members. They in turn share their ideas on how to make it happen, and the team drives it through.

I've had the privilege of working with Microsoft for many years as a productivity speaker, trainer, and coach. One of my clients is Mike Howard, Chief Security Officer for Microsoft, who recently explained how this shift occurred in his organization.

> A decade ago, we were creating three- to five-year plans and trying to map those out top-down. In the last few years, we've moved toward a one-year plan. We map out our priorities, accountabilities, and the execution strategy year after year, regularly updating it to match reality and course-correct if necessary. It's now all the same process.
>
> Some multiyear projects may bleed over, certainly, into other years. For example, I challenged my team to drive a social media strategy for global security. One of my groups has been executing off that, and certainly, that's a multiyear plan. I set the general parameters of where we should be going and get the buy-in from the leadership team.
>
> Usually, we do that through a couple of off-site meetings a year, along with our monthly Strategy Sync meetings. We map out current and new strategic priorities and how to move forward at the same time. Then it's up to team members to actually execute off this strategic vision. As they do, the strategy takes shape. We see opportunities and move quickly toward the best ones. The only time I would ever reengage in that process of their execution would be if I saw something going in the wrong direction. That's rarely the case. I provide the overall vision; team members actually figure out how to get there.

Workers have actually been innovating in this way for many years, but leaders haven't always been good at asking for it or realizing it. They're now saying, "Wow, maybe I'll just get out of their way and let them take me where we need to go." As Mike Howard pointed out, there must still be a leader to articulate the vision—that is, leaders should set the priorities—and workers should tell them how to get there.

The Modern Business Leader's Job

> Listen to the folks who execute, make their work easier, and support them in continually finding and pursuing new strategies.

> As leader, you're the disturber, the cheerleader, the coach, and the #1 supporter of your team.

> You enable your team to lead the charge.

As a leader, it's up to you to design a culture in which your people are willing to step up and take that initiative. Most workplaces, no matter how enlightened, still require a great deal of work to create such a culture, and thereby instill the needed behaviors to make this change. But that work is necessary, even critical, because it all comes down to this: your team must be free to determine how to best achieve success. That means they need the tools, training, and guidance to achieve well-defined success criteria.

Speed

I hardly need to point out how much faster the business environment changes today than it did even a few years ago. In response to the speed of change, workplace strategy needs to evolve much faster now than in the past. Achieving maximum results requires faster goal-setting and organic strategic execution. Your commitment to fostering agile, adaptive execution will make it easier to reshape organizational priorities in the moment.

For example, my office manager, Becca, recently attended a webinar on online strategy for small businesses. In typical Becca fashion, she immediately shot me a memo with what she learned and what we should do. For example, the presenter pointed out a current trend of using photos to reflect brand and personality versus the old staid headshot. Instead of asking permission, Becca took the initiative and sent me a meeting invitation with an appointment with our photographer for a photo shoot. ("Is she trying to tell me something?" I wondered as I accepted.)

The webinar presenter also said our websites should be relationship-oriented, mobile, and commerce-ready for handheld devices. In our one-on-one meeting later that week, Becca briefed me on the changes we were making to our site, outlining her plan in ten minutes. She would direct our marketing consultant to work on the site map, ask our IT guy to outline the move to WordPress, and get three proofs from the designer to review. I asked her the price tag, blinked, and gave her the thumbs-up. And that was it.

From a tactical perspective, a new "eureka" opportunity may suddenly bubble up and alter the focus and time expenditure of your strategic plan. One of my strategic priorities is to "Build The Productivity Pro, Inc. brand." I didn't know our company's website needed an overhaul to support that strategy, but *boom*, we're executing Project Revamp Website. This didn't happen because "it was time to do strategic planning." Rather, a team member made the decision organically when it became obvious a tactical change was necessary to support the strategy.

She came to me for resources and approval, and I got out of her way.

As a result, I had to push other tasks back in favor of this new project—that's where your team often needs your support. Periodically, leaders get together for a reality check on direction based on the movement in their areas. They share what they're working on, adjust the course if needed, and take off again.

Admittedly, because I head up a small firm, I can make decisions independently and turn on a dime, so my team can execute more quickly than a Fortune 500 company can. However, my clients in large corporations want to model this nimbleness, because it's absolutely necessary for their success. Don't just tell me, "That's the way it is around here." Nothing makes me crazier, and nothing fails faster.

Here's what leaders must tell their team members: "When you think of a great idea or come face to face with a new opportunity, don't wait three weeks to tell me about it in our next meeting. Get on the phone with me now." If you do a good job communicating the vision, their thoughts and actions begin to align with your organization's strategic objectives. Empower your team to act quickly! Never be too busy to hear about an idea or an improvement.

Validity

The best leaders have a vision for the future, which arrives daily. To quickly implement great ideas, you must do these two things well:

1. Identify the strategic priorities that will drive the business forward.

2. Take action on them quickly by leveraging your people and resources.

A huge caveat: You still must have a viable strategy, one that can actually achieve quantifiable goals within your constraints of time and cost. You also need to keep an eye on how well it's working, so you can refine your course as needed.

For example, as an author, the demise of Borders bookstores in late 2011 saddened me. What happened? Unlike its competitor Barnes & Noble, Borders failed to properly account for the risks presented by online book distribution. It's not that Borders didn't have a strategy; its strategy just didn't work well. The changes were coming, the writing was on the wall, and its leaders recognized the need for a strategic shift. However, they chose a bad strategy. No amount of fast action will get you out of trouble if you're speeding in the wrong direction. Clearly, Borders simply couldn't react fast enough. It stood by watching as other companies nibbled on the edges of its market and ultimately shut it down.

The Bottom Line Is Simple

> There is no shortage of good ideas.

> It's not about who has the best ideas.

> It's about who executes their good ideas best.

FOUR KEYS TO EFFICIENT STRATEGIC EXECUTION

THE L-E-A-D FORMULA™

L = LEVERAGE

Do you have the right people and drivers in place to achieve your strategic priorities—ones that allow you to execute your strategy when the rubber hits the road? If not, you have a talent/resource issue.

E = ENVIRONMENT

Do you have the organizational atmosphere, practices, and culture that will allow your employees to easily support your strategic priorities? If not, you have a cultural/ engagement issue.

A = ALIGNMENT

Do your team members' daily activities move them toward the accomplishment of the organization's ultimate goals? If not, you have a communication/productivity issue.

D = DRIVE

Are your organization's leaders, teams, and employees agile enough to move quickly once the first three pieces of this list are in place? If not, you have a speed/agility issue.

FOUR KEYS TO EFFICIENT STRATEGIC EXECUTION

After more than twenty years of helping leaders create high-performance cultures and accelerate growth, I've identified four crucial factors that must be in place for a leader to execute strategy efficiently. Without these elements, execution can fail—even when you base it on a mature, effective strategy. The four keys to efficient strategic execution—Leverage, Environment, Alignment, and Drive—represent solutions to these failures and form the L-E-A-D Formula outlined in this book.

The L-E-A-D Formula represents the real-world implementation of interdependency, fluidity, speed, and strategy (the four premises outlined at the beginning of this introduction) as they relate to on-the-spot, flexible strategic execution.

Most leaders find their organization is weak in one or two areas. The Execution Quotient Assessment that follows this introduction will help you determine which of the four keys you need to strengthen in your own individual business. The assessment shows you where to find the information in this book. When I'm invited to speak at a corporate meeting, I ask the audience members to take the assessment online, so I can compile the cumulative scores. When the audience sees the perceptions of the overall group, its leaders can take action as a whole.

LEADERSHIP ROLES AND DEVELOPMENT OPPORTUNITIES

Each of the four keys to efficient strategic execution has a corresponding leadership role and development opportunity that can be seen in the following chart.

LEADERSHIP ROLES AND
DEVELOPMENT OPPORTUNITIES

L

LEVERAGE

Leadership Role
Engineer: Build It

*Development
Opportunity*
Talent/Resources

E

ENVIRONMENT

Leadership Role
Mechanic: Fix It

*Development
Opportunity*
Culture/Engagement

A

ALIGNMENT

Leadership Role
Conductor: Steer It

*Development
Opportunity*
Communication/
Productivity

D

DRIVE

Leadership Role
Bulldozer:
Knock It Down

*Development
Opportunity*
Speed/Agility

ORGANIZATION OF THIS BOOK

The L-E-A-D Formula's four keys correspond with the four sections of this book, to help you readily identify which key might represent your biggest leadership challenge. Each section has three chapters, so if you hosted a book club with your team, you could discuss the book in three months (see www.ExecutionIsTheStrategy.com for complimentary discussion and leader guides).

Key 1: Leverage explores how to employ the concept of leverage to apply a stronger force as a leader, strengthen your "levers" (employees), and improve your "fulcrum."

Key 2: Environment explores the importance of shaping an agile, responsive organizational culture, encouraging change hardiness in your team members, and engaging employees.

Key 3: Alignment shows you how to convince team members to care about your goals, define what those goals will be, and determine how to get there.

Key 4: Drive focuses on your team's path to productivity. It includes how to remove obstacles from their paths, speed things up, and remove time wasters.

Keep this in mind: Leaders should work with their people to build effective business strategies in real time. You may not have time for strategic planning as such, but you should always make time to build an organizational culture that's adept at strategic execution.

By the time you finish reviewing each of the four keys, you'll see that execution really *is* the strategy that will propel your organization forward in today's fast-paced business arena.

▶▶ Visit **www.ExecutionIsTheStrategy.com** to receive complimentary bonus material, videos, articles for reprint, worksheets, and book club materials. ◀◀

The Execution Quotient (EQ) Assessment

The purpose of this EQ assessment is to provide insight into your current strategic execution process as you prepare to read this book. The assessment is organized by the four sections of the book, corresponding to the keys of the L-E-A-D Formula™. Each chapter and question has a focus that is highlighted in bold and repeated in the scoring section.

After you take the assessment, transfer your scores to the following Score Sheet to analyze them further. You can also take the assessment electronically at www.Execution IsTheStrategy.com and e-mail the results to yourself.

TAKING THE ASSESSMENT

Answer each question using the following scale:

1 = to no extent
2 = to a small extent
3 = to some extent
4 = to a considerable extent
5 = to a great extent

KEY 1: LEVERAGE

Chapter 1: Maximize Your Input Force (Leadership)

1. To what extent do I **delegate** my authority as effectively and widely as possible? Do I refrain from doing what others on my team are capable of doing?

   1   2   3   4   5

2. Do I guide and oversee the work of my team? Do I avoid micromanagement and demonstrate **trust**?

   1   2   3   4   5

3. Do I lead by example? Do I **model** the behaviors I expect from others?

   1   2   3   4   5

   SUBTOTAL _____

Chapter 2: Strengthen the Beam (Employees)

4. To what extent do I identify and hire high-performance workers? Do I know what attributes are needed to meet my future **talent** requirements?

   1   2   3   4   5

5. Do I take the time to **coach** my team members? Do I connect them with experienced mentors?

   1   2   3   4   5

6. Do I consistently provide my team members with the **training** they need to increase their personal performance? Do I invest in my key talent?

   1   2   3   4   5

   SUBTOTAL _____

Chapter 3: Improve the Fulcrum (Resources)

7. To what extent do I provide my team with the **equipment** they need to do their jobs better? Do they have the right technology?

1   2   3   4   5

8. Do I emphasize **cross-functional thinking** among my team members? Do we work to coordinate goals with other departments and employees?

1   2   3   4   5

9. Do I outsource tasks that others can do more inexpensively or effectively? Do I seek **partnerships** to "fill in the blanks" with expertise I lack?

1   2   3   4   5

SUBTOTAL _____

KEY 2: ENVIRONMENT

Chapter 4: Shape the Culture

10. To what extent do I foster an environment of **excellence** on my team? Do I encourage everyone to always give their best?

1   2   3   4   5

11. Do I build a firm foundation of **accountability** in my team? Do I emphasize the importance of reliability?

1   2   3   4   5

12. Do I encourage a **collaborative** atmosphere within my team? Do I embrace mutual learning and community to maximize success?

1   2   3   4   5

SUBTOTAL _____

Chapter 5: Encourage Change Hardiness

13. To what extent do I embrace change as it occurs
    and roll with the punches? Do I actively seek out
    openness and usher in change?

    1   2   3   4   5

14. Do I create a nonpunitive climate of **risk-taking?**
    Do I encourage innovation and creativity?

    1   2   3   4   5

15. Do I emphasize **continuous improvement** for
    myself and my entire team? Do we always strive to
    get better?

    1   2   3   4   5

    SUBTOTAL _____

Chapter 6: Ensure Engaged, Empowered Employees

16. To what extent do I drive engagement among
    my individual team members? Do I encourage people
    to take **initiative?**

    1   2   3   4   5

17. Do I reinforce our **joint** responsibility to accomplish
    our team's goals? Do I demonstrate how individual
    output contributes to everyone's success?

    1   2   3   4   5

18. Do I empower my employees to **own their jobs?**
    Do I provide them with what they need and get out
    of the way?

    1   2   3   4   5

    SUBTOTAL _____

KEY 3: ALIGNMENT

Chapter 7: Take Your Team on a Mission

19. To what extent do I understand what **motivates** each team member to perform at a high level? Do I understand that people contribute discretionary effort for different reasons?

    1   2   3   4   5

20. Do I show genuine **appreciation** for hard work? Have I discovered what would be meaningful to each person?

    1   2   3   4   5

21. Do I keep a clear picture of our goals in front of my team? Do I continually **communicate** excitement for our mission?

    1   2   3   4   5

    SUBTOTAL _____

Chapter 8: Plan for Goal Achievement

22. To what extent do I establish clear performance **expectations** for each person? Do team members know precisely what they should be doing?

    1   2   3   4   5

23. Do I work with my team to establish a plan to achieve our workplace goals? Is our **project planning** and management seamless?

    1   2   3   4   5

24. Do I ensure that the day-to-day operations of my team will achieve our long-term goals? Do we merge strategy and **tactics**?

    1   2   3   4   5

    SUBTOTAL _____

Chapter 9: Measure Your Progress

25. To what extent do I tie each person's goals into our
performance management system? Do we track
the accomplishment of individual goal attainment?

           1   2   3   4   5

26. Do I measure my team's performance at regular
intervals? Do we jointly **review our key milestones**
on a routine basis?

           1   2   3   4   5

27. Do I create advance plans for potential crisis?
Do I prepare for **contingencies**?

           1   2   3   4   5

SUBTOTAL _____

KEY 4: DRIVE

Chapter 10: Remove Obstacles from the Path

28. To what extent do I remove the obstacles that slow
my team's execution? Do I work to clear **roadblocks**
when necessary?

           1   2   3   4   5

29. Do I reinforce the need for **urgency** and efficiency?
Do I encourage my team to "turn on a dime"?

           1   2   3   4   5

30. Do I **make speedy decisions**? Do I keep over-
collaboration or perfectionism from slowing us down?

           1   2   3   4   5

SUBTOTAL _____

Chapter 11: Add Enablers to the Equation

31. To what extent do I help my team members eliminate workplace distractions? Do I give them time to think, be strategic, and **focus**?

    1   2   3   4   5

32. Do I create team **protocols** to ensure efficient communication? Do we follow consistent guidelines for instant messaging, e-mail, and conference calls?

    1   2   3   4   5

33. Do I work to **eliminate** activities that fail to support our strategic priorities? Do I understand that what we don't work on is as important as what we do work on?

    1   2   3   4   5

    SUBTOTAL _____

Chapter 12: Eliminate Time Wasters

34. To what extent do I encourage team members to accomplish tasks in order of **priority**? Do I keep people focused on results, not activity or busyness?

    1   2   3   4   5

35. Do I spend **meeting time** productively? Do I keep attendees focused and stick to the agenda?

    1   2   3   4   5

36. Do I encourage a reasonable **work/life balance**? Do I understand that overwhelmed people hit a point of diminishing returns?

    1   2   3   4   5

    SUBTOTAL _____

EXECUTION QUOTIENT SCORE SHEET

Copy your scores and subtotals from the previous sections and add them up to find your grand total. See the scoring categories below to interpret your score.

KEY 1: LEVERAGE

Chapter 1: Maximize Your Input Force (Leadership)

1. Delegation _____

2. Trust _____

3. Modeling _____   SUBTOTAL_____

Chapter 2: Strengthen the Beam (Employees)

4. Talent _____

5. Coaching _____

6. Training _____   SUBTOTAL _____

Chapter 3: Improve the Fulcrum (Resources)

7. Equipment _____

8. Cross-functionality _____

9. Partnerships _____   SUBTOTAL _____

                                     KEY 1 SUBTOTAL _____

KEY 2: ENVIRONMENT

Chapter 4: Shape the Culture

10. Excellence _____

11. Accountability _____

12. Collaboration _____   SUBTOTAL _____

Chapter 5: Encourage Change Hardiness

13. Openness _____

14. Risk-taking _____

15. Continuous improvement _____   SUBTOTAL _____

Chapter 6: Ensure Engaged, Empowered Employees

16. Initiative _____

17. Joint goals _____

18. Job ownership _____   SUBTOTAL _____

KEY 2 SUBTOTAL _____

KEY 3: ALIGNMENT

Chapter 7: Take Your Team on a Mission

19. Motivation _____

20. Appreciation _____

21. Communication _____   SUBTOTAL _____

Chapter 8: Plan for Goal Achievement

22. Expectations _____

23. Project planning _____

24. Tactics _____   SUBTOTAL _____

Chapter 9: Measure Your Progress

25. Performance management _____

26. Review milestones _____

27. Contingency plans _____   SUBTOTAL _____

KEY 3 SUBTOTAL _____

KEY 4: DRIVE

Chapter 10: Remove Obstacles from the Path

28. Roadblocks _____

29. Urgency _____

30. Decision making _____   SUBTOTAL _____

Chapter 11: Add Enablers to the Equation

31. Focus _____

32. Protocols _____

33. Elimination _____   SUBTOTAL _____

Chapter 12: Eliminate Time Wasters

34. Prioritization _____

35. Meetings _____

36. Work/life balance _____   SUBTOTAL _____

KEY 4 SUBTOTAL _____

GRAND TOTAL: KEYS 1–4, QUESTIONS 1–36 _____

Scoring Categories

151–180: **Congratulations!** You have a deep and effective understanding of strategic execution and know how to achieve it. All you need to do is fine-tune a bit. Keep up the good work!

121–150: **You need a few tweaks here and there.** You're on the right track! Strive to improve any question where you gave yourself less than a "5." Give yourself credit for what you do well and acknowledge where you can improve and save even more time.

91–120: **Average.** You're "middle of the road," which isn't bad, but it's a bit boring. You're not the worst, and you're not the best. But who wants to be average? Work on kicking up your strategic execution efforts a notch, so you can get more done and produce stellar results!

61–90: **Major overhaul required.** You'll need to get serious about changing the way you handle your strategic execution, from setting goals through strategy to execution. Stop working so hard on the wrong things. Select one item on this list every two to three weeks and work on systematically improving your competence level.

36–60: **Danger!** Your productivity and strategic execution skills need a jumpstart, stat! Both your job and your organization's future may depend upon it, so start working hard on the right things right now.

How to Use Your Scores

Compare your total scores for each section of the book to determine which L-E-A-D factor is the weakest link in your process. Within each particular key, you can delve deeper by comparing the chapter subtotals, thereby better understanding which topic you've expressed a weakness in. Even more useful is looking at the individual questions within each chapter for the lowest scores; in fact, those represent your best places to start. This is very much a bottom-up method of continuous improvement (another concept I focus on in this book).

As you study each chapter, especially those where you've scored poorly, think about how you can improve your process. If your weakest part of the L-E-A-D Formula is Leverage, where does the greatest weakness fall: in Leadership, Employees, or Resources? For example, if you've got a full slate of 5s except in the Resources chapter (chapter 3), where you drop to 4 on Equipment, 2 on

Cross-functionality, and 3 on Partnerships, then it's clear where your first efforts at improvement should lie: with Cross-functionality. Make a sincere effort to think beyond your desk, to break up information silos on your side of the divide, and to reach out to other groups in a collaborative, mutually beneficial manner. Then you can start working on your Partnership flaws, before polishing up the Equipment issues, gradually bringing everything up to a 5.

Once you're happy with your new results, move on to another unsatisfactory function and work on bringing it up to par. While I would normally tell you to focus on improving what you're already good at—that is, pushing your scores from good to great rather than wasting time on things you don't do well—the functions I discuss in this book represent exceptions to that rule, because these are the conditions under which successful execution can flourish. They're so fundamental that they require the maximum level of competence you can bring to bear, in order to strategically execute on the spot so well and so automatically that you ensure the survival of your team.

As you put new concepts successfully into play, return here occasionally and retake the assessment to determine how much you've improved. You should see improvement relatively quickly, and you may not recognize that original you a year from now.

Leverage

1

L
LEVERAGE
Leadership Role Engineer: Build It
Development *Opportunity* Talent/Resources

When I was a kid, my younger brother Paul—who later graduated from college with a degree in mechanical engineering—taught me how using a lever could make building a snowman easier.

My father is a retired Air Force colonel. I grew up on the Air Force Academy in Colorado Springs, so I'm used to snow and lots of it. I remember one particularly big snowstorm that closed school and delivered perfect snowball-making snow. Paul and I naturally decided to make an enormous snowman.

We started with a huge base. Then we rolled a middle snowball nearly as large, and quickly discovered it was so heavy we couldn't lift it. So my clever brother grabbed our Radio Flyer wagon and a wooden 2 × 8 beam from my father's shed. Using the wagon as a fulcrum and the board as a lever, he lifted the middle snowball onto the base snowball while I guided it. After that, finishing our snowman was easy.

In the strictest mechanical sense, a lever is a simple machine with a rigid beam that pivots on a fulcrum or fixed hinge to magnify an input force, so the resulting leverage or output force can move heavy objects.

The concept of leverage fits equally well in the workplace, where applying it can facilitate smooth, on-the-spot strategic execution. The same basic components of leverage used to move a snowball apply to any business system. You can leverage physical and financial assets, experience, skill sets, specialized knowledge, and relationships to get the right people in the right roles. This means using the right tools to squeeze every bit of productive work from your team. It's also the epitome of learning to do more with less—a powerful principle in today's resource-poor workplaces.

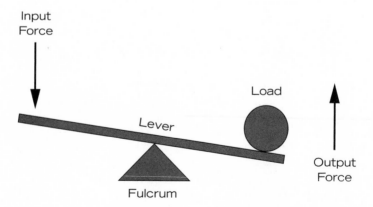

An efficient organization is one that operates with leverage already in place:

- • The Effort/Input Force = the leader (you)
- • The Lever/Beam = the worker (employee or team)
- • The Fulcrum/Pivot = the enabler (tool or resource)
- • The Load/Object = your organization (what you're trying to move with your strategy)

The interaction of these components is said to create leverage. Depending upon the strength of your strategy, the leverage created (the output force) can move the object (your organization). If the interaction of this simple machine with its component parts creates enough leverage, your organization will move where you want it to go. Without the right parts in place, movement will be much more difficult.

Put another way, the ability to lift the "snowball" in your organization requires increased input force. This is achieved either through a stronger leader, a longer and stronger beam (team members), or a fulcrum of more appropriate size, height, or position (tool or approach), or perhaps even a lighter snowball.

You'll find it well worth the effort to develop or acquire the authority to leverage your resources and assets at will, not to mention those of your allies and partners. Why? Having the ability to apply the right amount of force at just the right time allows you to take advantage of fast-moving opportunities that may knock only once.

LEVERAGE IN ACTION

My two sons Johnny and James love to eat at the Chick-fil-A near our home. So I was delighted when Roger Blythe, Vice President of Business Analysis at Chick-fil-A, called upon me to work with his team at an upcoming department meeting.

When we chatted about the concept of leverage, Blythe told me,

> There's a lot of conversation around here about how to move more quickly. Even though we're not under the pressure of bad financial results, we do constrain ourselves around the resources that we add every year. Our desires to continuously improve and add new features and services typically exceed the resources we can add in any given year, so there's a built-in mechanism that forces us to try to become more efficient.
>
> In my own area, we try to create as much clarity as we possibly can about the goal and what we're trying to accomplish. Then we hire wonderful people—really smart, bright people who are engaged—and we give them a large amount of freedom and flexibility in executing that plan.

When you have the right people in the right roles and the right tools in place, the leverage gained makes implementing your strategic priorities far easier. So don your engineer hat, and let's explore ways to build this simple machine so you can help your team execute with greater agility.

Maximize Your Input Force

As Archimedes once said, "Give me a lever long enough and a fulcrum on which to place it, and I shall move the world."

How do you get more power into your lever? Simple. You have to be a stronger leader. But what, precisely, does that mean in today's world? Not what it once did, that's for certain. The modern era's simpler information exchange, better communications, and increased mobility have altered perceptions of leadership in interesting ways.

Motivational expert Ken Blanchard points out, "In the past, a leader was a boss. Today's leader must be a partner with their people. They can no longer lead solely based on positional power."

I couldn't agree more. Modern leaders can't afford to be autocrats, because by the time they decide on a strategy, it's usually out of date. No single individual can keep up with everything in real time. Instead of trying to, the intelligent leader delegates his or her authority as effectively and as widely as possible, encouraging both risk-taking and creativity. That allows the team to transform the organization from within.

Think of it this way: as a leader, you work for your team members. They don't just work for you, although the organizational chart may suggest otherwise. Don't think of yourself as belonging to a different class than your team members just because the categories seem so clear-cut on paper. You all relate to each other along a continuum rather than as separate boxes. (Rare exceptions occur in high-security situations or during war, when compartmentalization is required.)

So why bother even having a leader? Because you need someone to articulate and guide the team's mission and vision. The modern leader exists less to tell people what to do than to urge them to do what they already know they should. Rather than controlling every worker's daily activities, you serve as a nucleus for your team members to rally around. You're a catalyst triggering ideas and action, allowing people to succeed without getting in their way.

Let's consider a few of the many ways you can maximize your input force.

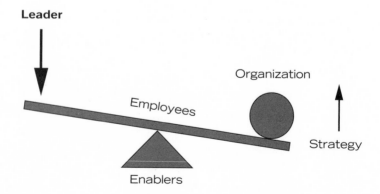

GIVE YOURSELF A HAND!

You have a staff for a reason. Ideally, each team member on your staff possesses talents, knowledge, and abilities that combine to form the extra hands Mother Nature didn't give you.

Speaking of hands, here's a helping HANDS approach to keeping your team properly aligned with organization strategy—without tipping you over the edge into overwork.

1. *Handpick your people.* Select each with an eye for the skill set he or she brings to the table, aiming for a little overlap with other team members, but without too much redundancy. Once they're on board, get to know them well. Determine their weaknesses and strengths, consider how they might work best together, and decide which tasks should go to whom.

2. *Assign duties carefully.* Meet with your team leads and parcel out the range of tasks they have authority over. Define the limits of their authority carefully to avoid duplication, but make sure there aren't any cracks for tasks to fall through.

3. *Nurture initiative and innovation.* In a memorable scene in the 2011 film *Captain America*, a sergeant tells a group of soldiers out on a run that if one of the men can retrieve the flag from atop a tall flagpole, he'll get a ride back to the barracks. After several soldiers fail to climb the pole, wimpy Steve Rogers takes a look at it, pulls a pin at the base, and pushes it over with his foot. He retrieves the flag and trades it for his ride back to the barracks. Give your people the opportunity to surprise you with their solutions to tasks you assign.

4. *Don't abdicate!* Delegation is not abdication. Carefully consider how much authority to delegate with

the responsibilities you parcel out, but never give it all away. Keep a high-level eye on both team and individual workflow. Intervene if someone doesn't live up to expectations or fouls the works. Do whatever you must to repair an individual's productivity before the whole team's productivity falls apart. As the leader, you bear the ultimate responsibility for every team member's success and failure.

5. *Study the results.* Has delegation reduced your task list to a manageable length? If not, intensify your efforts. Resolve to handle only the high-value items you do best or must do as part of your job. In addition, determine how your delegating has affected the team's workflow process. Do you have a well-oiled machine on your hands, or does it move forward in fits and starts? If the latter, rethink who does what and how, and clear the obvious blockages.

Delegating work forms the backbone of any managerial time management strategy, so learn to do it well. You can multiply your hands and extend your brain, thereby accomplishing much more than you ever could alone.

JUST SAY NO TO YOUR INNER CONTROL FREAK

Having a forceful personality provides certain advantages in a competitive workplace. It can help you work your way up the ladder more quickly than you otherwise might. But fair warning: if your favorite management slogan is "my way or the highway," expect a few delays in your drive to the top.

You can survive with this attitude, but nobody loves a control freak. Your team will never give you 100 percent if you disempower them, hover over their shoulders, or constantly disparage their abilities or judgment. They will either resent you or get so nervous they won't be able to do their jobs correctly. And if you're always poking into their business, you won't get your job done, either.

Control freaks in leadership positions crush creativity, drive depression, and kill camaraderie. All of these weaken your lever's input force. Worse, they also block the kind of frontline development and immediate execution of strategy that success depends on. So let's check on your micromanagement tendencies. Read through these questions carefully and answer them honestly.

- Do you often find yourself standing over employees' shoulders directing their work?

- Do you regularly redo employees' work, even as a form of "instruction"?

- Do you second-guess your employees' decisions on a daily basis?

- Do you require an approval or sign-off on every task, even minor ones?

- Are you convinced of the truth of the old saying, "If you want something done right, you've got to do it yourself"?

- Do you work twelve-plus hours a day?

- Do you recheck the work of those you're responsible for?

- Do you have a hard time focusing on the big picture and drown in minutiae instead?

- Do you get involved in little $12-per-hour details?

- Are you insatiably curious, so much so that you just have to know what's going on behind the scenes?

If you answered "Yes" to more than a couple of these questions, then you have micromanager tendencies. You must fight them! If you answered "Yes" to many or all of them (or pretended you didn't), then I have bad news for you: you're already a micromanager.

Micromanaging drives a stake through the heart of employee productivity; it's as simple as that. It's as much about fear as it is about control. Micromanagers are not necessarily on a power kick; rather, they mistrust everyone. They're afraid if they don't "ride herd" on the team, everyone will make catastrophic errors. Afraid of the consequences of letting go, they hold on to as much of their power as they can.

The result? You create a stifling environment, in which both your time and the employees' get wasted. Micromanaging fails right up and down the line. Not only does it exhaust everyone involved, it's ultimately counterproductive and drives away the best workers.

Furthermore, even when done with the best of intentions and the lightest of touches, micromanaging interrupts people. If you poke someone a half-dozen times a day and ask how far they've gotten on an assignment, you can't expect them to get very far. When they have to answer you, it drags them out of their focus. In fact, employees often tell me their manager is their biggest distraction, always swooping in and checking on them, rendering them unable to get anything done.

Given that, where do attention to detail, intelligent oversight, and high professional standards break down and mire you in the trap of micromanagement? It all hinges on trust. When you surround yourself with competent, well-supported people and trust them to do their jobs, micromanaging isn't a problem. But when trust goes out the window, micromanaging springs up like a weed. When lurking and criticizing happen incessantly, both productivity and employee morale go down the drain.

A REAL-WORLD EXAMPLE

I once did training for the vice president in charge of the call center at a large telecom company. She cited overwork and burnout on her team and called me in to help.

Upon further exploration, *she* proved to be the biggest culprit. I know this seems like common sense, but many leaders simply can't see how they're contributing to crazy-making. It quickly became clear why this vice president felt she had no time to think about strategic issues. She insisted on attending meetings that were also attended by the director and manager of that department. She had employees copy her on every e-mail about issues they were resolving internally with customers, so she'd be "in the know."

Clearly, it's unnecessary to have three levels of management represented in each meeting. The vice president should excuse herself, release the appropriate level of authority to her managers, and instruct them to report the results. (Unfortunately, no one was recording action items, because everyone was in attendance.) She should explicitly tell those she trusted to resolve customer escalation issues without copying her on e-mails. She only needed to know about the results in the closeout ticket.

THE BIG T: TRUST

How do you develop the level of trust in your employees that's required to inspire productivity and empowerment? I believe it starts with self-awareness. If your organization suffers from low productivity, don't automatically blame your employees; take a look at yourself first. If you don't trust your people to do their jobs well, ask why. Did you make poor choices when you hired them? Are you still learning how to maximize their skills and abilities? Are you paranoid someone will take your job? Have you failed to provide the proper training? Realize that if your involvement is so crucial to your current role that you're irreplaceable, then you can't be promoted. That's why you should always be grooming a successor.

As the architect of your team, it's up to you to choose the right materials for the job and put them together in the most structurally sound way. So in ridding yourself of your micromanaging tendencies and bringing your organization up to snuff, your first task (ironically) may be to take an even closer look at your team members and their abilities. Assess how each contributes and what you can do to maximize those contributions. Then develop an action plan to train or coach them to increase their productivity, thus tightening their fit in the general workflow of the organization.

You may find it necessary to replace individuals who aren't doing well enough, just as you would put aside low-quality tools in favor of better ones. While that may sound cruel, if a few have advanced beyond their competence level, you can't keep covering for them. After all, that's what micromanaging is all about—trying to do others' jobs because you think they can't.

The truth is, you can't afford to waste time or energy watching over those who are already supposed to know what they're doing. If you delegate responsibilities appropriately, prepare your employees for their jobs, and give them everything they need to do them, you won't need to ride them. Trust that they can do their work, wind them up, and let them go. Show them you have faith in their ability. You won't be able to execute strategy efficiently if you don't.

If they're unworthy of your faith, then, yes, you'll have to take corrective action, which is for the best. Even if you fear someone might fail when faced with certain job challenges, trust in that person to have the ability to solve those challenges. How else can they ever learn and grow?

When you rely on your employees and prove they can rely on you to back them to the hilt, you'll establish a high level of loyalty and discretionary effort. At the same time, make sure the organization's mission, vision, and goals are clear to everyone. Set basic ground rules, determine who reports to whom and how, and then turn your attention to your own tasks. Learn to trust—but verify.

How much do you need to verify? That depends on an employee's previous performance, experience, and skill level. Basically, though, if you've done all you can to bring competent people on board, your role is simple. Believe in them and let them do their jobs, checking in occasionally and correcting course as necessary.

When you hire capable, engaged people and trust in their competence, you've got the enviable position of being a hands-off manager. If they know what they're doing, it doesn't matter how they do their jobs, as long as they do so legally and ethically. If they need advice, trust that they'll ask. If certain employees show signs of falling flat on their faces, let them. They'll either learn quickly or wash themselves out due to incompetence. Be encouraging, yes, but know that you can't do everything—or even most things—for them. That way can be ruinous for all involved.

Remember, when you trust, you're not abdicating your responsibilities; you're simply using other people's talents to get things done. Trust is the heart of delegation. As a leader, you don't just represent another layer between consumer and product. Rather, you direct and expedite the workflow, while providing the resources necessary to stimulate performance.

BARKING ORDERS
IS NOT COMMUNICATION

Once trust becomes a permanent part of your methodology, your biggest challenge will be how to communicate priorities to those on your team. This may require different levels and types of communication for each person; again, it's up to you to determine what's best.

Sometimes leaders get so busy running around, dashing off e-mails, and barking directions that they completely fail to communicate. If you don't get the need for communication, let me assure you, your employees do. And here's what they'd like to say to you about it.

1. *Listen.* Start taking the opinions of your teammates seriously. Don't assume you always know better than they do. Success comes more easily when you leverage other people's experience, skill sets, relationships, and creativity. Don't expect to have all the right answers.

2. *Talk.* Get to know your team members on a personal level, so you can better understand their motivations. Speak to them openly and show that you value their roles in achieving the organization's strategic goals. Be sure to overcommunicate priorities: you can't tell them what you expect of them too often or too much.

3. *Let go.* Leadership isn't about retaining every bit of power. You may be loaded down with responsibilities, but your leaders expect you to pass on most of your

assignments to others, so do so. Then, within the limits of their authority, let your subordinates delegate some of their duties. That helps make everyone accountable for the success of the team.

4. *Get back to work.* As a leader, you have a duty to provide direction, set priorities, and work toward goal alignment along with the rest of your organization. If you try to do that along with everything else, you won't be able to do any of it well. So start trusting people to do their jobs while focusing on your own strategic priorities. Measure your personal progress by the movement of the team itself, not a to-do list of firefighting tasks that someone else should take care of anyway.

What's your true talent as a leader? It lies in your ability to recognize what to do to encourage, support, and motivate your employees so they can execute effectively and efficiently—without strangling their initiative or engagement in the process.

SHOW THEM THE WAY (EVERY DAY)

As a leader, you're also a teacher—both in the leadership-by-example sense and in the instructive sense. As Ralph Waldo Emerson once said, "What you are speaks so loudly, I cannot hear what you are saying." Employees learn partly by watching you and partly by receiving instruction. Unless you're a spymaster or a military commander, never ask anyone to do what you aren't willing to do yourself. That includes behaviors such as:

1. *Arriving late and leaving early.* Ever had a boss who rolled in at 10:00 A.M. and then left at 4:00 P.M., after telling everyone to stay late to hit the big deadline?

I suspect you didn't find that inspiring. Don't demand excessive hours on key deadlines if you won't put them in yourself. But on the opposite end of the scale, if you regularly work twelve-hour days, don't expect people to work as long as you do unless there's a valid reason. Long hours do not contribute to greater productivity.

2. *Sitting back during emergencies.* Sometimes you'll need to lend a hand to prevent the team from being overwhelmed. So rather than hang back when your people are floundering, offer to help. When an unexpected challenge emerges, rise to it. Put your back into it until you meet the deadline. Obviously, don't make a habit of pitching in; save it for crunch-time and emergencies, or you're back to micromanaging.

3. *Playing favorites.* You'll inevitably like some employees more than others, but you can't let favoritism sway you. Dole out discipline and rewards when people deserve them, whoever they may be.

4. *Not practicing the Golden Rule.* Treat others with respect and dignity, the way you'd like to be treated. The leader who builds buy-in through polite direction engages the workforce more effectively than the one who bullies people.

As a leader, you set the gold standard and must remain above reproach—not just most of the time but all the time. Otherwise, why should anyone listen to a thing you say? While we're all fallible human beings, leaders are held to a higher standard and must work hard to achieve a decent balance. Still, some leaders go off track, so keep a good head on your shoulders and be willing to roll up your sleeves whenever the circumstances warrant.

THE FINAL WORD

I recently heard a word used I'd never heard before and had to look it up: "defenestrate." (In general, I recommend eliminating words from your vernacular that people have to look up. It's not impressive; it's annoying.) Defenestrate means to throw a person or an object out the window. Now that you know the meaning, it's appropriate to apply it to what you have to do with many long-term business strategies as they grow stale.

In some industries, any strategy more than a few months old is outdated by the time it reaches the people who actually make things happen. That means you have to move rapidly from idea to execution or risk eating the competition's dust.

As the leader, you shape the overall vision for your team, communicate and agree on tactics, and let your team take it from there. Don't adopt a purely hands-off approach, but don't micromanage either; that's a recipe for catastrophe. Your people need the freedom to do their jobs as they see fit. Trust them to tell you what they need to do to achieve your vision. That's where true leadership lies—not in strait-jacketing your people with inflexible rules and hidebound strategies.

Now that you've maximized your leadership input force using the methods described here, let's move to the next part of the leverage equation: strengthening and lengthening the beam—your team members.

Strengthen the Beam CHAPTER **2**

To move more weight with a lever, you either have to apply more input force, improve or reposition the fulcrum to magnify the output, or strengthen the beam so it can handle more strain. In chapter 1, we looked at the input force. This chapter looks at the beam, while chapter 3 addresses the fulcrum.

To strengthen the beam of your organizational lever, you need the right people in place, armed with the right skills needed to execute in the moment. As Steven Gangwish, Vice President of CSS Farms, told me,

> The question of *do we have the right people in place* comes up with every project. It's not just incremental—we might be adding a new potato farm—so it's not just about adding one or two people. We can add ten people at a time for new projects. It's kind of the chicken and the egg; you can't take on new projects without the right people, but it's hard to support the right people without the new projects. In the past, I think we've erred on the side of being too lean. Our model is to get the project rolling, and then we try to find the right people.

At times, that has been cost effective for us. But it has also been a hindrance in terms of taking advantage of all opportunities—because ultimately, you're short on people. Generally, we try to staff projects within our organization. The way we offer more responsibility and professional growth to our existing people is by pursuing business growth opportunities they can help lead. The downside is that it often means a relocation, and that's not always the easiest thing to do.

Janie Wade, Senior Vice President of Strategic Financial Planning and Analysis at Baylor Health Care System, echoed the challenge of having the right people in the right places at the right time for the right projects.

We have a talent planning process that is renewed frequently—at least annually. It has the elements of traditional succession planning but is focused more on who we have coming up the ranks, what strengths they have, and what types of projects they need to perform to be ready to move into a different role.

How do you know if you have the right person? Let's look at a few criteria you'll need to consider.

HARD WORK VS. TALENT—WHAT'S THE SCORE?

The concept of equality is a cornerstone of American culture. While some people may be born into better circumstances than others, we all have equal rights to life, liberty, and the pursuit of happiness. In fact, we've enshrined that in the documents that declare and outline our system of government.

But as equal as people may be in the eyes of the law, it would be a mistake to assume or assert that all people are the same. Certain abilities come more easily for some people than for others. We simply can't doubt the existence of the elusive quality called talent.

Recently, the *New York Times* reported that, all else

being equal, the "profoundly gifted" tend to do better in life than their less-talented colleagues.[1] That makes sense, but so do the studies suggesting that, in the long run, hard work and practice can overcome a lack of natural talent— indeed, that they often take people farther and higher than talent alone.[2] Like the nature vs. nurture debate, this discussion may drag on for decades before reaching any consensus (if it ever does).

When it comes to human intellect and behavior, pat answers rarely exist beyond children's stories. Perhaps "practice makes perfect" comes closest to reality. Research by psychologist K. Anders Ericsson (popularized by author Malcolm Gladwell) estimates that it takes about ten thousand hours of practice to become an expert at anything.[3] This applies most obviously to music and sports, but it also extends to mundane activities like applying business skills, writing well, driving a vehicle, and even doing housework. We just don't celebrate these things the way we do Yo Yo Ma's cello playing or Michael Jordan's basketball skills.

For every Mozart who excelled as a child prodigy, we have an Albert Einstein, who did only reasonably well at math in school but later became the world's best-known physicist. Consider Tiger Woods, who started playing golf at the age of two and became a superstar in the sport by the time he was eighteen years old. Does Woods have talent? Indubitably. Did the right opportunities and many years of practice hone his talent to a keen edge? Absolutely.

If talent trumped hard work, then would the most famous basketball player in history have started out on his junior varsity high school team? Well, he did. Michael Jordan's coach didn't even think he deserved to be in his school's top ten players. Jordan undeniably has talent. However, combining talent with hard work and pushing himself well beyond the required workouts got him into the Hall of Fame.

The lesson? Talent does provide an edge—you can't deny that. But more than talent is required to maximize success.

**Hard work beats talent
when talent doesn't work hard.**

When it comes to success,
I believe three qualities hold
greater value than sheer talent: **hard work**,
                                        persistence,
                                        and **DESIRE**.

Your best bet for maximizing strategic execution, then, is to have hardworking, flexible people with a combination of talent and experience in the places where they can do the most good.

HIGH PERFORMER OR AVERAGE WORKER?

Adding a new person to your workplace team is always a gamble. Usually you can't tell by looking who will consistently deliver top-notch performances that make the entire team shine—as opposed to who will just show up and do an average job.

Realize that "average" does *not* mean "bad." As I discuss in my book *SuperCompetent*, average (competent) people define the norm and provide the benchmarks by which we recognize high performance.[4] They do their jobs adequately when directed, and you can depend on them for most things.

But you build your team around high performers—the "quantum leapers" who achieve up to ten times greater results than the average worker. Slow and steady may win the race, but you need to hitch yourself to a star to make real progress.

So how can you detect this star quality? Look for these attributes.

1. *Stars look good on paper.* "Paper trails" offer clues about people's performance ability. Did someone graduate summa cum laude with a double major? Good—that suggests an overachiever. If someone has quickly risen through the ranks at previous jobs with stellar performance records, you may have a winner on your hands. But you can't always rule out the possibility of a personality or attitude change since that last glowing review.

2. *The Yoda attitude.* I love the line by Yoda, the little green Jedi master in *Star Wars*, who told Luke Skywalker: "Do. Or do not. There is no try." Look for this attitude during your face-time interviews with each candidate. High performers confront workplace challenges head-on and apply experience and creativity to craft tailored solutions that get the job done. Ask candidates what they'd do in hypothetical situations, noting how well and how quickly they can construct a reasonable solution.

3. *Sharp, well-defined goals.* High performers have no problem citing their goals, both short- and long-term. They can present those goals neatly and quickly and show a solid understanding of the steps required to achieve them. They know how to translate goals into action.

4. *Ambition.* High performers push themselves to get ahead. These high-energy self-starters radiate confidence, don't need anyone else to motivate them, and maintain a clear sense of direction.

5. *Excellent time-management skills.* High-performance burnout can be a big problem. Ambition, solid goals, and a can-do attitude matter little if a worker can't juggle time well. High performers understand the basics of time management well enough to create a work/life balance that maximizes their personal productivity without exhausting themselves.

You've probably experienced an occasional pleasant surprise when someone you've written off as average suddenly rises to the top of the performance ladder. Similarly, you may have suffered disappointment at the hands of a "sure thing." In the end, performance matters, not appearance, so take care not to mistake style for substance.

Search for the five characteristics outlined here before assuming you have a firecracker on your team. "Masters of disguise," who depend on their winning personalities to get them on board, usually can't hide their weaknesses well enough to evade careful scrutiny. True high performers exhibit a fearless, ambitious, action-oriented and—above all else—results-oriented approach that no one can easily fake.

FILL IN THE BLANKS

However you define the right people for a particular task, you'll likely find a need for further seasoning before they can handle all the input force you'll bring to bear. One way to accomplish this is through mentoring.

According to legend, when Odysseus left Ithaca to fight in the Trojan War, he left his son Telemachus in the capable hands of a teacher named Mentor. In the millennia since Homer wrote *The Odyssey*, the concept of the mentor has become deeply ingrained in Western society.

We generally perceive a mentor as an older individual who takes someone younger under his or her wing, passing down knowledge in a nurturing relationship that benefits them both. Today, an age difference isn't considered as important as it once was; what does matter is the experience transmitted, along with the relevant patterns of thought.

In the business environment, mentoring is often a hit-or-miss prospect. Opinions on the topic tend to fall into two categories—either mentoring would be nice to do if we had the time, or it's a complete waste of time. But effective mentoring is never a waste. In fact, it can boost the productivity of both the mentee and the mentor significantly. When it does, mentoring contributes to the success of the entire organization.

Mentoring becomes a productivity accelerator only when an organization takes it seriously—that is, when it becomes more than an educational tool indulged in "as time permits." Productive mentoring drives performance and challenges mentees to grow into their roles in profitable ways. If you undertake it in a half-hearted way, at best you'll get half-hearted results.

You should also approach mentoring as an exchange, rather than a situation where the mentor simply dispenses knowledge to the mentee. The teaching method should be largely Socratic—that is, asking rather than telling. To encourage initiative, present challenging, even provocative questions. For example, questions to ask in a mentoring situation might include:

- What do you think we should do to accomplish this goal?

- Can our current workflow process handle this situation?

- If you were in charge, what would you cut or add?

- What would you recommend to solve this problem?

- If you were a competitor, what would you hope we would do wrong?

- What would you hope we wouldn't do?

- What can we learn from our competitors in this situation?

- How would you respond to this situation if you lost a key person?

- Could you recover easily if you lost that person?

- What is your plan if you're hospitalized for several weeks?

And so on. The often surprising results are always worth exploring—not only because they stretch the mentee's abilities and get him or her to think independently, but also because they help instill the concept of personal accountability.

Certainly, mentors should lay the groundwork with basics such as organizational rules, structure, and expectations of the mentee's role within the company. They should also impart lessons learned and provide unique perspectives on the business environment, politics, and culture. But otherwise, rather than simply provide answers, mentors should challenge mentees to succeed by teaching them *how* to think, not *what* to think.

Mentors must also have the authority and flexibility to allow their mentees to try and fail. Will some mentees fail to rise to the challenge? Of course, but even then the results can be productive if they illustrate shortcomings in the mentee's training and abilities. In fact, that's another function of mentoring: identifying the mentee's strengths and weaknesses. Because leaders expect certain minimal levels of performance in any position, they can teach employees what to improve on and how to do it through constructive mentoring.

Good mentoring also builds connections among the various levels of an organization, helping mentored individuals expand into their roles and providing opportunities for further growth. This contributes to a valuable esprit de corps that improves morale. Part of this strategy involves the mentor exploring the mentee's frustrations and worries, and then suggesting ways to overcome them without directly fixing them. Maximizing the employee's potential and productivity is the goal.

Not surprisingly, all of this requires collaborative communication. The mentor should make it clear that candid feedback is not only encouraged but required. In particular, the mentee must be willing to ask questions (especially when something is confusing) and become self-aware, receptive, resilient, and willing to grow.

As a leader, when you make mentoring a priority in a productive, challenging way, it can provide significant value to everyone involved.

TRAIN TO MAINTAIN THE STRAIN

A beam can break if it lacks sufficient strength, and strengthening your team requires having a framework in place to allow instant action. While technological competency should be a given, I can't overstate the importance of training and continuing education.

For starters, don't ask an employee to do something he or she is incapable of or untrained to do. Ideally, training should be goal-oriented and used in conjunction with mentoring (see the previous section). Provide the necessary training to overcome any limitations, including:

1. *Legal and ethical training* (at a bare minimum).

2. *Technical training* to help people become proficient in their day-to-day jobs (systems, databases, software, etc.).

3. *Personal and professional development* to help them become better performers and know how to:

   - Handle e-mail more efficiently.

   - Think strategically.

   - Improve communication skills with colleagues.

   - Run meetings more effectively.

   - Prioritize better and become less reactive.

   - Focus on high-value work instead of procrastinating.

4. *Skills training* for capabilities they might need in the future.

Perhaps the last one—the skills training—gave you pause. Why would you invest money training people for something they don't need and may never use? Because strong leaders look at the current skill sets of their team members and consider their future needs months or years down the road. They recognize when they don't have the right people on board to meet upcoming strategic needs. But maybe they have the right people with the wrong skill sets, so they need to train them up now to be prepared when that time arrives.

Debbie Gross, Chief Executive Assistant of the Office of the Chairman and CEO at Cisco Systems, notes the importance of becoming adaptable by having skills ready at a moment's notice to move into a new space. She said,

> In today's world, you have to have a multiple number of skills that allow you to be marketable—that let you jump from one job you may have had for years and years to another.
>
> In the administrative world, I see professionals who do the same thing every day, because they've been doing it the same way for twenty years. They're not really open to utilizing new technologies. If for any reason their boss leaves or retires, they're sitting there without the skills to be marketable anymore.
>
> I'm not a technology wizard by any means, but I think one of the key elements that keeps me going is the curiosity of how something can help me. What could this do for me? How can it benefit me in the future, both personally and professionally? Curiosity is the seed.

During his one-on-one meetings with his leadership team, Cisco CEO John Chambers strives to understand his

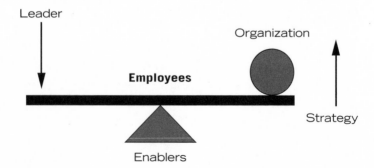

employees' career goals. He wants to know where they've been in the company, what roles they've had, what their desires are, where their strengths are, and where they need to develop. Debbie Gross told me, "He wants to get into a deeper level in terms of who they are as individuals, as opposed to managing that piece of business. Once you understand who they are as individuals, you can play to their strengths. If they're a great runner, you put them into a position where they can run. If they're a great bruiser, like in football, then you put them in the front line."

The lesson here? Keep working on building the skills your team members will need in the future. Play to their strengths; don't worry as much about developing their weaknesses. As a leader, discover each person's talent and bolster his or her confidence. Then you'll be able to put each of them where you need them down the line, so you can go even faster and strike harder.

THE FINAL WORD

It's up to you to strengthen an employee's ability to execute strategy in every way possible. Keep these pointers in mind when improving your organizational "levers":

- Look for and reward hard work over talent. If you find people who have both, snap them up immediately and treasure them.

- Learn to recognize the difference between high performers and average workers at a glance.

- Mentor newbies to help them learn the ropes.

- Provide the training your team needs to execute more effectively.

Once you've strengthened your beam, find a way to improve your fulcrum, as discussed in the next chapter.

Improve the Fulcrum CHAPTER **3**

A fulcrum is the hinge or pivot a beam acts against to multiply the input force. In the real world, it may be a handy rock, a log, or the bar a seesaw pivots on. If you use the right size, height, and position for your fulcrum, you'll be able to get more leverage from your system.

Equipping your team members with the right tools, such as computers, software, and the Internet, can strengthen their leveragability. A business fulcrum may also consist of anything from specific productivity approaches to professional relationships.

While this topic alone could consume a forest's worth of books (and no doubt has), in the interest of brevity, I'll present only a few examples of tools, resources, and approaches.

EQUIP YOUR TEAM FOR SUCCESS

Provide your team members with the tools they need to succeed. In my onsite seminars, employees frequently complain about their various systems, their software, and related company policies. A common complaint is that the company does not allow them to load personal software onto their computers; another is that the company places restrictions on accessing certain Internet sites.

Some policies are justified. Allowing personal software can create a legal issue in the financial industry or a headache for the IT staff if workers want help on non-company-supported applications. This practice could also create security concerns and open the door to system viruses. And I can't think why employees would need to watch X-rated content at work.

On the other hand, employees' complaints about other policies are well founded. For instance, many people prefer having their own local printer, so they don't have to walk down the hall to pick up printouts—yet the company denies them this option. I frequently print long documents because I get headaches when I read them on the screen. Also, some people like to take a paper copy of a document to a meeting to mark up and discuss, or print handouts for

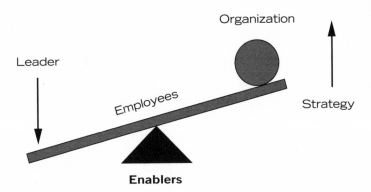

an upcoming presentation, or print a specific document for easy reference.

It's crazy to multiply the amount people make per hour by the number of employees in an organization walking down the hall to the shared printer (and potentially wasting time with Chatty Suzy). Plus, what often happens? You get to the printer and find it didn't print your file, or someone took your print-out by accident, or the result isn't what you thought, or the margins are cut off, etc. So it's back to your office to print again.

The cost of buying and servicing local printers is minor when compared to the lost productivity of using shared printers. So if those on your team believe their time and organization would benefit from having a dedicated printer, oblige them.

Ditto for people "who aren't at a level where a smartphone is authorized" or are told, "you can't connect your personal device to work e-mail" or "you can't import your Google calendar into Outlook." Huh? You have employees who want to check work e-mails on their personal time and better balance their lives, and you won't allow it?

Legalities and firewalls aside, people are far more productive when they have access to their e-mail, calendar, tasks, and contacts from anywhere whenever they want it. It's a time-waster to send yourself e-mails from home or leave yourself a voice mail, just because your time-management system is inefficient or deliberately crippled.

If employees are willing to dip into their pockets to buy a device that aids their workplace productivity (and thus increases the profitability of the organization), give them permission to connect into the system; better yet, buy the devices yourself. Get in touch with the reality of how employees operate today. My administrative assistant has her own smartphone, and I certainly allow her to check her work e-mail on it.

People don't turn off their private lives when they walk through the work door. Similarly, they don't stop thinking about work while at home, either. Face it: you can't have it both ways. If people maintain two unconnected systems, it weakens their ability to manage their time well and sets them up for conflicts and inefficiencies, which can damage your team's performance and the speed at which each person can execute.

THINK BEYOND YOUR DESK

In 1988, Peter Drucker predicted that within twenty years most organizations would readily coordinate and share tasks across all levels. This "cross-functional approach" would increase response time for the customers' benefit. As visionary as he was, Drucker missed the boat here. While most modern business schools do emphasize this approach, relatively few real-world organizations practice it in any meaningful way.

Team-first functionality is typically the norm. Despite paying lip service to organizational mission and vision, modern business structure encourages leaders to carve out individual fiefdoms rather than foster seamless integration across departments. As a result, leaders often experience informational silos, turf wars, and internal sniping—quite the obstacle for strategic planning.

Chick-fil-A has found a way around this. As Roger Blythe told me,

> A lot of our planning used to be siloed. But about ten years ago, we recognized the need to coordinate at least the big strategic pieces. We actually put a planning leadership team into place. At one point, the team had an officer-level representative from every department, but it got a little unwieldy. We made it work for five or six years, but we recently moved to a smaller team that doesn't have complete functional representation.

The challenge to members of that group is to take off their functional hat and put on their big-picture, strategic-thinking hat. They've all been at Chick-fil-A for at least ten years. Their task is to think about the big picture for the organization and recommend big-bucket, strategic directives that ultimately our most senior executive team—what we call the executive committee—will endorse and bless. This planning strategy team also has the responsibility to allocate budgets accordingly.

This strategy reminds me of being on the board of directors for the National Speakers Association (NSA); indeed, adopting this quasi-internal board strategy could keep your team and organization from succumbing to myopia. You can also SEARCH for better ways to align your team's efforts with the overall organizational objectives:

1. *Share.* Information silos occur when information gets stuck within one group. Sometimes the group deliberately hoards it; sometimes it results from incompatible systems between divisions or departments. Either way, silos cost businesses billions of dollars per year. Make sincere efforts to communicate and share critical data laterally across teams and departments.

2. *Empathize.* Are you so focused on your team's needs that you've lost track of the organization's goals? Stop and think about the needs of other groups, and consider how much more you and your co-leaders might accomplish (or how much rework could be saved) if you actively helped each other. Think about how any action or decision will impact another, and talk about it before you pull the trigger.

3. *Appreciate.* Instead of belittling Human Resources or Accounts Payable for how little their accomplishments matter compared to your group's, try to understand and

appreciate each area's contribution. The organizational chart includes those functions for a reason, even if it isn't obvious to you.

4. *Respect.* In addition to understanding and appreciating other teams, learn to respect what they do. Reach out and connect with them, so you can better serve each other. When feasible, attend their big meetings so you can gain knowledge of their inner workings and needs. Find ways you can reduce redundancy or even save them time.

5. *Change.* Mutually beneficial relationships founded on sharing, respect, and appreciation drive cross-functional thinking, which in turn drive organizational flexibility and a stronger bottom line. Do everything in your power to encourage a shift to cross-functional thinking. Emphasize how moving forward with a more holistic strategy is in everyone's best interest.

6. *Heal.* Sure, the old-school functional methodology gets you by—the same way a crutch does when you have a broken leg. But isn't it better to have two healthy legs? Functional thinking is prone to brittle self-absorption, causing breaks across the organizational structure. Open, honest cross-functionality helps reset those breaks, so everyone can move forward more easily.

As Mike Howard of Microsoft commented in our interview,

> Sometimes you have to force cross-functional thinking to speed things up and avoid rework and conflicts. I've stressed something over the years called SI or Strategic Integration. SI has been part of our yearly commitment for many years now. When someone from my leadership team comes up with a strategic idea, it is transparent to everybody else. We can see

areas of convergence and potential areas of conflict, which allows us all to march in the same direction from a strategic point of view.

If two members of my team are crosswise on a particular project, they must talk through it, so their team members aren't creating bottlenecks for others in our organization. Nine times out of ten, they can work it out; if they can't, they come to me, and I'll make the decision.

If the bottleneck is an external issue, however, and another part of the organization is keeping my folks from executing, then it's up to me to intervene. Who's in the right posts, and what are the leverage points I need to tap? What other general manager or senior leader in that particular organization do I need to sit down with to say, "Here's an issue that's keeping us from moving forward. What can we do to collectively solve this problem?"

SHARING MEANS CARING

In his comments, Mike stressed inclusivity, meaning it's all the same organization, not "us versus them." So be sure to ask, "What benefits both sides?" Leaders should recognize the impact of their work on other departments. They have a high-level perspective of company-wide workflow, whereas individual contributors can't always see the links. Plus, when you make an effort to build trusting relationships over time, others will be more willing to help when you come to them with issues. This can help events move forward more quickly.

Good cross-functional teams consist of people representing the right mix of different departments, disciplines, and functions. By combining their efforts, they can achieve the function or meet the goal that drove the team's formation in the first place—whether that involves speeding up product development, providing a quick turnaround on customer requirements, or deciding how to divide this year's bonus pool fairly.

Without good cross-functional communication—and a lot of common sense—some people lose track of what truly matters. I've heard of military quartermasters who withheld much-needed items from soldiers on the front line for bureaucratic reasons. They were so focused on operating their little fiefdoms that they forgot the overarching organizational goal: to win the war.

Instead, by sharing goals and data, you can break down information silos and successfully integrate your actions with other departments. Further, if each group knows every other group's goals, everyone can work together to identify areas of overlap and devise ways to eliminate redundancy, thus saving the company money.

For example, suppose two or more groups in the company are regularly compiling the same set of reports. Wouldn't it be more profitable to eliminate that redundancy by centralizing production of those reports with a single group?

Getting members from different teams together to break bread can also cross-pollinate ideas and boost the creative process. Mike Howard of Microsoft explained, "For the high potentials on my team—the direct reports of my leadership team I call my kitchen cabinet—I have several mechanisms. Once a month, I meet them for a kitchen cabinet lunch, and we just socialize. I also meet with them on a monthly basis, and each of us takes turns talking about our business issues and processes."

At some point, you'll face a choice on your organizational path. You could keep following the well-traveled dirt road of team-first functionality, but doesn't it make more sense to take the yellow brick road to a cross-functional future? After all, those yellow bricks may be made of gold.

The cross-fertilization and new viewpoints that emerge from true teamwork can prove insanely profitable, so unleash cross-functional thinking in your working life and improve your team's potential success.

DELEGATION IN THE GLOBAL VILLAGE

While delegation is a prerequisite for productivity at the leadership level, certain activities aren't worth your team's time. For instance, when the copy machine breaks down, your highly paid Linux coder shouldn't be attempting to fix it. Hire someone else to do it!

This process of hiring outsiders, formally known as outsourcing, allows you to leverage your people and resources more effectively and profitably.

Businesses have been outsourcing work to other businesses since the beginning of the modern era, if not longer. Consider subcontracting, a venerable practice, which is actually a form of outsourcing. When you hire someone to fix the roof, wire an electrical outlet, handle the coffee service, or carry a package across town, you've just outsourced some of your organization's work.

Many companies also outsource their information technology, customer service, and accounting. In fact, you can outsource almost anything. And you should, because outsourcing simply makes sense. While it has its flaws, it can help you increase your efficiency and lets you connect with a flexible pool of specialists in a particular field, reduce risk, cut capital costs, limit overhead, and, most important, concentrate on your core business.

Outsourcing also allows you to tap other people's knowledge and skill sets without having to take them on full-time. You use them as you need them—a real bonus when dealing with short-term projects or peripheral functions you don't need a full-timer to handle. In tough times, outsourcing also makes it easier to streamline your team without loss of function. It leaves some of your strategy-as-execution to consultants who, having helped multiple clients over relatively short-term time frames, bring speed and agility to your organization.

Sources of Outsourcing

Given the growth of international currencies like the Euro and simple online payment providers like PayPal, you can easily reach out and hire people halfway across the planet if they seem the best choice for a particular service. When you do, you'll want to know where to find these long-distance team members, so let's look at a few options.

Certain web-based entities act as global employment platforms, clearinghouses where workers bid on projects posted by potential buyers. The process offers benefits for both sides, but in many ways, the buyers have the upper hand. Most projects attract dozens of bids, so you can carefully pick and choose from the respondents. You'll also get a variety of prices, ranging from a specific baseline (set by the platform) up to amounts that may seem astronomical. The global nature of the platforms can allow you to choose economical providers because you're able to tap technical experts in countries that have lower costs of living than where you live.

If a worker fits your needs and provides quality work on time, you can make him or her a permanent part of your virtual office and eventually bypass the clearinghouse altogether. If that person doesn't work out, you can sever the tie and hire someone else. These clearinghouse sites work much like brick-and-mortar employment agencies, but with greater transparency. I'm listing a few here.

Elance.com has been around in one form or another since 1999. One of the largest of the virtual-worker clearinghouses (if not the largest), it has more than 1.4 million registered contractors as of this writing. You can post projects in a wide variety of categories, including copywriting and translating, virtual assistants, computer coding, and more.

Guru.com also traces its origin back to 1999 and works

in a similar way, though it doesn't claim quite as many contractors. Other virtual-worker marketplaces similar in style and execution to Elance and Guru are Freelancer.com and oDesk.com.

Some of these platforms specialize in specific types of virtual worker, with the structure varying from site to site. But all provide access to a global pool of potential employees—and most don't charge the buyer a cent. Experiment to find which one fits your needs best, and move forward from there.

Outsourcing Considerations

Approach outsourcing as another business decision, treating it as you would buying computers or office supplies. Calculate the best deal and implement it confidently. Remember, though, that the cheapest choice isn't always the best; after all, you don't buy a two-dollar watch if you want something you can rely on for accuracy and durability.

These days, when I realize my current staff doesn't have the bandwidth to manage a particular task or project that suddenly popped into my mind, I immediately log into Elance.com and have someone working on it within a few days. I sort my options by feedback score, number of reviews, location, and tested skill level, so I'm confident I'm picking the best person for the task. I've rarely had a bad experience with anyone I've hired online.

Let me reemphasize that outsourcing doesn't have to be limited to platforms like Elance or oDesk. Steven Gangwish of CSS Farms told me, "We use a lot of outside consultants for our agronomy. Rather than have a bunch of Ph.D.s on staff who know everything about plant pathology and entomology and so forth, we use university and outside consultants to leverage that capability and have state-of-the-art knowledge."

GET BY WITH A LITTLE HELP FROM YOUR (VENDOR) FRIENDS

"In the farming business," says CSS Farms' Steven Gangwish, "you can't just add a customer and get twice the sales."

> You can't roll out a new product and your business exponentially grows. It's more of a stair-step growth model in terms of people, assets, and capital. If you want to add a new farm, you just don't do it overnight. One way we have overcome that in the last several years is to partner with another company. We are really good at growing potatoes, and we know a lot about it, and we're efficient at it.
>
> We don't know a lot about marketing to grocery stores and the retail chains. For us to build that experience and capability and hire the right people would be a big uphill battle. Instead, we partnered with a company on this new venture that has the existing marketing expertise, and were able to build that business essentially overnight. Now we're in over ten thousand retail grocery stores selling our products.

Obviously, the synergy in a case like this can be a lot more than 1 + 1 = 3. Look at your expertise and at what you do well. Rather than hiring new people to fill in the blanks, look around and find someone who already does what you need.

BEFORE YOU TIE THE KNOT

Before you take on a prospective business partner at any level—as a contractor, vendor, or full-on partner—ask these seven questions:

1. *How well do our strategic priorities align?* Aligning strategy within one organization is hard enough, much less between two or more. The better your missions match, the more likely you'll be able to leverage off each other. But don't expect a slam-dunk; other factors

may stifle synergy. For example, the animal advocacy groups PETA and ASPCA have similar goals, but their tactics differ drastically, so they probably wouldn't make good strategic partners.

2. *Do we both have strengths we can leverage?* Don't dismiss an organization out of hand just because it's bigger or smaller than yours. Instead, look for what you can each bring to the table that maximizes everyone's productivity and profits. Sometimes individuals can successfully partner with organizations consisting of thousands of employees because each side wants what the other side has.

3. *Are we in direct competition?* If you offer complementary products and solutions that fit hand-in-glove or function in non-overlapping geographic areas, you can leverage a business partnership effectively. Otherwise, it's extremely difficult (remember the failed merger of the telecommunications companies Nextel and Sprint?). You can join the same industry groups, but you can't expect to partner well with organizations competing for identical resources.

4. *Will they provide access to pre-established relationships?* The easiest way to acquire profits, working capital, and influence is to leverage existing relationships with clients and contacts. A new partner can let you take advantage of existing relationships you don't have to build and might not ordinarily be able to access.

5. *Do they have relationships I value?* Take great care in the selection process. Make sure your prospective partner's existing relationships represent the type of relationships you're looking for. Similarly, be careful whom you introduce to your own contacts and clients,

since a bad partner can damage your existing business relationships. If anything seems fishy, back off.

6. *Can we multiply each other's efforts?* In some cases, the right partnerships can put you in multiple places at once without increasing your workload, as with Steven Gangwish's example in the previous section. Suppose you and a partner agree to write guest blogs for each other. Right there, you've doubled your online visibility without increasing your workload or duplicating content. You can also share jointly written copy identifying all partners involved. That lets you multiply your exposure by the number of partners without multiplying your marketing expenses.

7. *What's my exit strategy?* If the relationship goes sour, you'll need a way to escape before you incur permanent damage. As you map out your strategies, devise a way to safely and fairly dissolve the partnership if it starts going in the wrong direction.

The value of teamwork is revered, but many organizations fail to consider opportunities outside their "immediate family." Rather than go it alone, consider developing ties with organizations independent of yours. Proceed carefully by asking the questions outlined here before you tie the knot.

Poorly considered partnerships can end disastrously. On the other hand, a good partnership, properly leveraged, can benefit you in ways you've never before experienced.

LIGHTEN THE FINANCIAL SNOWBALL

Remember that object you've been trying to move? If it only weighed less, the job would be a lot easier. Perhaps you can slim down the organization you need to shift.

Even though it took me a year and a half to earn my

MBA, I can summarize the issue for you in one sentence: To succeed, a business must make as much money as it can and save as much money as possible.

To make money, an organization typically applies these three strategies:

1. Attract as many new customers as possible.

2. Keep the customers it attracts.

3. Invest wisely in people, facilities, infrastructure, processes, and financial instruments like stocks and bonds.

To save money, an organization could implement any or all of these six techniques:

1. Reduce staff.

2. Reduce benefits.

3. Reduce salaries.

4. Reduce the quality of products and/or services.

5. Reduce expenses.

6. Increase productivity.

While viable and sometimes even attractive to misguided or desperate leaders, the first four techniques are difficult, because they can potentially damage the organization in the process. The fifth is reasonable (there's no need to waste money when you can save it instead); however, it's challenging to organizations that have already cut to the bone.

Number six is by far the best option. Rather than damage your infrastructure and reputation with false economy, find ways to tighten efficiency and increase team productivity instead. For example, if you have ten people on your team and can improve each person's productivity by 10 percent, then you now have the equivalent of eleven people—and you didn't increase salary expenses by one thin dime.

Hundreds of ways to hone productivity exist, but these are some of the most common methods:

- Eliminate unnecessary tasks.

- Rein in unproductive behavior.

- Focus on high-value tasks.

- Upgrade software for additional functionality.

- Purchase faster computers.

- Reduce interruptions.

- Cut back on meetings.

- Allow your team freedom to execute.

You have many options for saving money by increasing productivity. Done correctly, you won't need to make bone-deep cuts in staff, salary, benefits, and quality.

THE FINAL WORD

To take full advantage of leveraging, not only do you strive to strengthen yourself and your employees, but you may also have to replace or reposition your fulcrum to maximize your output.

So equip yourself and your team members with the right hardware, software, and resources. Think beyond your desk. Develop new partnerships, seek alliances, take advantage of outsourcing, and maximize your vendor relationships. Finally, be careful about what you cut. Short-term cuts that seem viable now could be disastrous in the long term. Rather than resort to any drastic measures, find ways to increase your team's productivity.

Environment

E
ENVIRONMENT
Leadership Role Mechanic: Fix It
Development *Opportunity* Culture/Engagement

Effective execution depends on establishing a productive, supportive work environment. In turn, a successful work environment depends on workplace culture. A company's culture guides discretionary behavior, picking up where the employee handbook leaves off. It's defined by what happens when the CEO leaves the room.

Ideally, you should encourage an organizational environment in which employees strive to "own" their jobs in the best sense of the word: they take initiative to align themselves with overriding strategic goals, pitch in enthusiastically, collaborate gracefully, and innovate without permission or fear of reprisal.

So, are you:

1. Creating a culture that helps employees feel confident, capable, and in control of the outcome of their work?

2. Building an atmosphere that encourages and accepts change?

3. Engaging and empowering people to do their work, without excessive oversight?

These critical environmental factors ensure commitment to the company's core mission and vision, which results in greater productivity over the long term. So don your mechanic's hat and get ready to fix anything preventing your team from achieving your goals.

Shape the Culture CHAPTER 4

Workplace culture largely depends on the unwritten ground rules and the attitudes of the members of that culture. Ideally, the underlying mood is positive, responsive, and energetic. Despite what celebrity pundits might claim, you can't just say you want your culture to be agile, accountable, and top-quality, and then expect it to happen. What matters most is the synergistic combination of attitude and action in the workplace.

FOSTER AN ENVIRONMENT OF EXCELLENCE

One of the strongest drivers for employee engagement is an employee's relationship with his or her manager. That being the case, what actions should you take to build that kind of relationship?

On a day-to-day basis, you want to motivate your team in positive ways—by walking the talk, leading by example, and making your personal integrity obvious and clear. Let team members know what you need them to do and when they've done it right (as well as when they haven't). With few exceptions, your employees want to get ahead and develop their skills, so help them. Be a leader in every sense of the word, making them realize they have a chance to excel under your leadership.

Also take into account diverse individual needs based on age, position, experience, and more. For example, someone new to the organization could be more interested in challenges and career growth, while better-established workers might care more about stability, rewards, and recognition. It's up to you to find out.

And don't be too quick to judge someone's motivation. A need for stability isn't necessarily complacency, and it's not a good idea to take advantage of this desire when the economy is struggling. Never base employee engagement on fear, even if it does seem to work for Darth Vader. Ask yourself this: When the economy turns around, how long will they stay?

Chances are, they'd stay if they worked for CSS Farms. As Steven Gangwish told me,

> When I think of the word *culture* and CSS Farms, one thing is for sure: if we're going to do something, we're going to be the best at it, almost to the detriment of profitability at times. If we're going to start a new farm, the mentality is that we're going to bring in brand new equipment, hire the best people, have the best land, and we're going to have the best customer, versus buying a used tractor to do that job, or renting this facility instead of building a new facility. There are pros and cons to both of those, but the employees really love working here. Excellence is something they can buy into. For better or worse, it provides a cultural expectation of excellence, and likewise, there is a demand of excellence from our employee base. They recognize that, and they respond to it, but they understand that part of the job is that they are going to do the best job possible. They are not going to do a halfway job.

You've heard the saying "the cream rises to the top," and anyone who's handled raw milk knows this is true. Business leaders love to apply this term to the workplace—but rarely do they bother to tell you that, with a little hard work on your part, your team's output can be *mostly* cream. Consider Jack Welch's General Electric, Lee Iacocca's Chrysler, or Steve Jobs' Apple, and, on a smaller scale, Ben & Jerry's Ice Cream (play on words intended).

Helping employees rise to the top takes time, careful planning, consistent guidance, and accountability. That's your challenge every day.

LAY A FOUNDATION OF ACCOUNTABILITY

In recent years, it's been easy to look around and wonder, "Whatever happened to accountability?" It often seems that both business and government are determined to rescue the worst troublemakers from the consequences of their actions—at public expense.

Consider the banking fiasco of 2008. Immediately upon receiving a huge government bailout check, AIG—which posted a fourth-quarter loss of $62 billion, the largest in history—awarded enormous bonuses to the very people who forced the bailout. Their excuse was that if they didn't award bonuses to their incompetent executives, they'd quit and go somewhere else. Perhaps that would have been best for the company.

To be fair, fifteen of the twenty highest-paid executives eventually agreed to return their bonuses, mostly because of the negative publicity. But a full quarter did not.

In real life, you reap what you sow, so work to instill and establish a culture of accountability in your workplace. Consider these five principles as you lay the foundation for accountability on your team.

1. *Outline the goals.* Your workers can't align their workplace efforts with organizational strategy if they don't know the strategy. Show them how their efforts move the organization forward and why positive productivity matters.

2. *Set expectations.* Agree on the worker's accountabilities. Clarify your performance guidelines and encourage them to meet specific goals.

3. *Set them up for success.* When someone needs training, tools, or continuing education to do their job better, make sure they have those things.

4. *Offer feedback, both positive and negative.* Never dress people down in public, but when they fail to meet your expectations, do let them know it. Also let them know, and let others know if appropriate, when they exceed your expectations.

5. *Inspire.* The original meaning of the word "inspire" was to quicken or animate—that is, to bring life to something. How do you inspire your people? Make your people proud of your leadership. Practice what you preach. Be equitable with everyone. Don't apply different standards to different individuals beyond the differences in their duties. Be a good role model. Be reliable and do what you say you will do. Behave in the same ways you ask of them.

Most people perform better when held accountable for their results. It's comforting to know you'll be rewarded for your hard work and that others on your team will be held accountable, too—because when you're part of a team, each member affects your productivity and schedule.

BUILD YOUR TEAM ON THAT
FOUNDATION OF ACCOUNTABILITY

When others fail to get answers to you, you may be late producing the final product. When you rely on coworkers to review a document before proceeding, a month can go by before you have everyone's input. As leader, then, it's in your best interest to help your team get things done more efficiently, so you can produce better results in less time and with fewer frustrations.

One way to increase everyone's responsiveness is to arrange a meeting with your team at the beginning of each project and plan it through to the end. I like to draw a big mind map on a whiteboard. Lay out milestones, responsibilities, and deadlines. You'll end up with a project outline (often called a work breakdown structure, or WBS), listing each person's deliverables, including yours. Build in contingency plans for potential crises.

If your team includes members in diverse locations, groups, or even organizations, negotiate clear agreements on when you need information, materials, or approvals. Explain your deadlines clearly, and ask when the member might be able to provide what you need. Reinforce the importance of what you're asking, and why their participation in the project is crucial. This may shore up their motivation, since we all like to feel needed and appreciated.

Contingency planning is especially important with team members you don't work with directly, so establish alternate means of acquiring what you need. That way, if your primary source happens to be away from the office or occupied by another project, you can turn to the backup person for help.

HANDLING BREAKDOWNS

Eventually, one of your team members will leave you in the lurch. Don't do their work for them or assign it to someone else unless it's a last resort or the situation absolutely requires it. Otherwise, you'll create a situation where they'll come to expect that, and, as a negative bonus, you'll inadvertently punish people for doing their jobs too well.

What comes next depends on several factors:

- Was the failure an oversight, or did the team member deliberately break a promise?

- Is this a one-time thing, or does it happen often?

- How badly did their failure impact the team's productivity?

Based on the relevant combination of factors, you have several options, which may escalate if the situation worsens.

1. *A gentle reminder.* Nudge them about the matter; you may jar loose what they've promised. This is the most common response in most situations.

2. *Make your displeasure clear.* If their failure has seriously compromised team productivity, or if this has happened more than a few times before, be more forceful.

3. *Have a talk with them.* If step two fails, schedule an earnest face-to-face meeting with them. Remind them of their promise and pin down a firm due date.

4. *The nuclear option.* If they prove they just don't care—or, worse, they think it doesn't matter if they lie to you—put them on notice.

If someone doesn't improve after repeated warnings and reprimands, you will have to let the offender go. You can't keep someone around who continually misses key deadlines. While personal productivity matters a great deal, most of us work in a team environment, so personal accomplishment must take a backseat to team accomplishment. Every person on a team, while not indispensable, is on the team for a reason. Therefore, they each have an obligation to do their personal best not just for themselves, but also for the team—and you, as team leader, have an obligation to hold them accountable for it all.

Never give up. With enough effort and the right tools, you can eventually build a voluntary culture of accountability in which you don't have to ride people to get them to do the right things at the right times.

INCITE A CULTURE OF ACTION

One of the prime forces in the universe is inertia: the tendency to stay either at rest or in motion. You can help people on your team overcome the "stay-at-rest" kind of inertia by giving them a boost, or, if necessary, a gentle nudge when they stagnate.

You can encourage a bias toward action by rewarding those who do the right things, as well as those who simply do things right. Simultaneously, coach others to change—and weed out those who won't, despite repeated opportunities. Poor performers drag down team productivity in more ways than one. Not only do they provide bad examples—"Hey, if Bob can get away with it, why can't I?"—they may poison good workers with their toxic attitudes.

Of course, you shouldn't punish people unduly when they make mistakes. They won't take chances unless you tolerate the occasional error; we all make mistakes. Besides, sometimes the best way to figure out something is through trial and error, what's often called the "Ready, Fire, Aim" approach. You try something, fix what went wrong, and try again. In warfare, this represents a standard artillery approach when determining range and connecting with a target.

The process of learning from what works and what doesn't also helps you spot potential leaders within your ranks. Identify the key personnel on the team and groom them for higher authority down the line. Urge them to share their thoughts, enthusiasm, and ideas with everyone. At the same time, you're supporting them, training them, and giving them the tools they need to do the job.

Have them educate the rest of your staff when you can't. This contributes to the all-powerful factor of job ownership, which motivates many people more than bonuses, promotions, awards, and perks.

PUNCH THROUGH THE BUREAUCRATIC MINDSET

Another way to provide dynamic, progressive leadership is to know in your bones what your organization does, why you exist, and whom you serve. You must understand not only the products and services you produce but also their benefits to the downstream user. Be aware at all times of your place within your industry and where the industry as a whole is going.

Furthermore, rather than allow a bureaucracy to petrify your organization, develop what futurist Alvin Toffler calls an "adhocracy": a series of ad hoc project teams and taskforces that handle specific projects directly, rather than allowing them to pass into the hands of planning committees or ill-prepared, overburdened managers.

ENCOURAGE A COLLABORATIVE ATMOSPHERE

In its most useful sense, collaboration simply denotes close-quarters teamwork—an essential condition for success in today's business environment. Ideally, your team already has a collaborative culture in place, but if it doesn't, do your best to foster one in the "many hands make light work" tradition.

"We have a very collaborative culture," says Janie Wade from Baylor Health Care System.

> We encourage people to work in multidisciplinary teams because we believe it results in better outcomes when people with different perspectives have input into a project.
>
> To avoid bogging projects down, we ask that the group agree on goals, timelines, and deliverables. Every two to three years, we do an all-employee survey to take a pulse on employee engagement. We get anonymous feedback on how well employees feel informed about our strategic priorities, and how well they feel connected to those priorities. Employees also have a place in the survey where they can tell us what they think works well and what they think needs to change. Following the survey, that feedback is incorporated into goals for the following year.

Good collaboration is apparent when you observe cooperative planning, a willingness to help, and consensus-driven decision making.

Cooperative Planning

Effective collaboration requires careful planning. Although it may be difficult to achieve, it's important for your team to strive to share the following on each new project:

- Common goals.
- Common metrics for measuring progress.

- A valued outcome.

- A firm deadline.

- A clearly documented, task-specific process.

- Sufficient resources, accessible to all.

- A clear division of labor.

- Unambiguous leadership.

Once the ball starts rolling, continue to build buy-in, solidify team spirit, and encourage group cohesiveness. True collaborative efforts require cooperation, commitment, flexibility, and a cheerleader (that would be you).

These efforts also require an investment of time—a scarce commodity, true, but achieving increased productivity makes it worth the outlay. Only return on investment (ROI) matters, not the initial cost. By harnessing others' labor, abilities, talents, and skills, you can maximize productivity all the way around.

Maintain a Climate of Mutual Help

Displaying a self-centered, me-first attitude slows everyone down. As a leader, you can't allow people to ignore the rest of the team. Don't let them establish their own fiefdoms, hoard resources, and build information silos. Instead, nurture an environment of free-flowing information, where individuals can step up and fix whatever goes wrong without running afoul of territorial disputes.

Make cooperation the standard, not the exception. This requires a shared perception that everyone in the organization makes up one big team, rather than discrete units that happen to be working toward the same general goals. True, organizational charts are necessary for structure, but attitudinally, you should try to erase the boundaries.

You'll also need to back your people whenever necessary, to maintain the climate of trust that makes mutual help practicable. Whatever you do, don't punish or ignore them when they raise concerns. Remember, the whole idea is for people to work together to reach the goals.

Drive Consensus

As a leader, you'll sometimes have to act unilaterally to get things done, without consulting your team members first. But often you'll want to take more time to think and gather others' input before acting.

When circumstances allow, consulting with team members and taking their concerns into account often represents the best way to achieve overall productivity. Before handing down an edict from on high, consider the merits of building a consensus for the decision you have to make first.

Some argue that consensus building has no place in business leadership, asserting that the workplace is not a democracy. But unless you work for an emergency service, why not adopt a few democratic tactics when making major decisions? This doesn't mean everyone should vote on everything; that takes too long. I've worked with some organizations that were *too* consensus driven; I was left with the sense of, "Just make a decision already!" But in general, sitting down with your team to consider all the permutations of an important decision makes good sense for a number of reasons.

First, many heads do work better than one. Consensus building lets you take advantage of the ideas, experience, and viewpoints of multiple individuals before deciding on a plan. Second, by sharing your authority, you give all team members a chance to play an active role in reaching the decision, which can ratchet up initiative. Watch them step forward and take a hand in achieving goals without your prodding.

So convene the team and outline the issues at hand. You might get the ball rolling by offering several ways forward, ticking off the positives and negatives of each. Encourage team members to contribute by making alternate proposals, asking clarifying questions, or raising objections. Everyone has a chance to voice his or her opinion and concerns, thereby shaping the direction the organization takes.

Consensus building works best when you let your team members make it their process, not yours. Your role? Act as a facilitator, not a dictator. Guide the process and keep it from losing momentum, but listen more than you speak.

It takes patience to build consensus, and it certainly doesn't work in every situation. It's a poor tool for handling emergencies, for example, because its thorough consideration of multiple options can take too much time. Some observers also reject consensus because it requires compromise, claiming everyone ends up unhappy. But that misses the whole point, which is to find a workable middle ground that allows the team to move forward as a unit. You didn't ignore the concerns of the individual members, so everyone can take ownership in the decision, even if they disagree with the outcome.

You'll find consensus building works best with small groups. But even if you lead a large team, you can use it to develop a basic framework for decision making by assigning specific types of decisions to certain individuals or sub-teams.

If pure consensus building doesn't work for either your situation or your management style, don't abandon the idea altogether. At the very least, bring your inner circle or leadership team together to advise you while you ponder your options. That way, even if the decision is ultimately yours and yours alone, you'll reach a better-informed conclusion.

THE FINAL WORD

Culture tells us how to respond to an unexpected situation. That might involve meeting an unprecedented service request, taking a risk by telling your boss about a new idea, or deciding whether to reveal or hide certain problems. Employees make hundreds of decisions on their own every day in the average organization. What guides them? The organization's culture.

Most senior managers struggle with the concept of culture because they find it difficult to define. Culture is like a cloud: you know it's there, but it's nearly impossible to grasp.

Wikipedia defines culture as "the set of shared attitudes, values, goals, and practices that characterizes an institution, organization, or group." But how do you come to a consensus—whether deliberate or unconscious—on those shared qualities? Even if you do, how do you get dozens, hundreds, or even thousands of people to think and act the way you've agreed on?

You don't. Culture is not a goal to be mandated; it's the outcome of a collective set of behaviors and unwritten ground rules you've inadvertently created or enabled over the years. Dedicate yourself to developing and rewarding desired behaviors, and let those rules guide your team as they meet change head on. Their weapon? Instant execution, because they know exactly what to do.

Encourage Change Hardiness

We've all experienced the "new broom sweeps clean" effect. We've watched, and often suffered, as a fresh leader came onto the scene and changed everything just because he or she could—regardless of how well the existing system functioned. Whenever this happens, chaos reigns and productivity plummets, and sometimes it never recovers. Then another broom soon appears to start its own ambitious cleaning project.

However, many changes are inevitable and even desirable. Otherwise, old inefficiencies may pile up until work grinds to a halt or the latest opportunity passes you by.

PEDAL TO THE METAL

To survive in business, you and your team must identify, understand, and respond to ever-accelerating change.

First of all, you have to come to grips with the inevitability of change. Nothing lasts forever. Help your team recognize and accept that change will always happen, like it or not. Given enough time, all things transform, wear down, fall apart, or burn out.

Denying and resisting change only causes pain. Adaptation to change, though, represents an essential life skill—the key to living without fear as you move forward to achieve your goals. It allows you and your team to respond creatively to the evolving environment. It also helps you maintain control rather than simply letting change happen.

You and your team may need to adapt to new technology, stay relevant to the new reality, and get ahead of competitors in both marketing and positioning. You've got to roll with the punches as they land, absorbing their momentum for your own use. This begins with a clear expectation of what will happen because of a new change. After that you set in motion an immediate search for the silver lining in what might, under other circumstances, seem like nothing more than a dark cloud.

Think of handling change as using your muscles. Your muscles will remain toned if you exercise them regularly, plus you can leverage the resulting flexibility and strength to improve your health. If you don't exercise, though, your muscles get flabby, leaving you open to injury when faced with a force you don't have strength enough to resist.

The same goes for your spirit and intellect. The more you limber them up, the better. Accepting and welcoming change expands your awareness, knowledge, and wisdom. At the same time, it broadens your overall perspective.

Whatever the changes you and your company face, be prepared to integrate them into your team structure so you can compete on an even playing field and pull ahead of the crowd. Constant changes bring new challenges for everyone from the C-suite on down, so learn from experience and adapt on the fly.

GREET CHANGE WITH A BEAR HUG

Charles Kettering, American inventor and former head of research at General Motors, reportedly once said, "If you've always done it that way, it's probably wrong."

As surely as hair grows and flowers bloom, change will come washing through your organization today, tomorrow, and always. Trying to resist that would be like trying to halt the tide. Remain alert to the possibilities in your surroundings, so an impending change doesn't pull the rug out from under you. Indeed, take advantage of it: catch the wave, hang ten, and use its energy to your benefit.

When a change approaches, rather than mire yourself in the mud of familiarity, learn as much as you can and encourage your team members to learn, too. Apply Walt Disney's famous dictum: Keep moving forward. Or, as Dory said in the movie *Finding Nemo*, "Just keep swimming."

If you can inspire the proper attitude about change, your people will react positively when it occurs. Start with these three basic tactics:

1. *Focus on the benefits.* Most changes won't devastate you. Instead of wringing your hands because the company has slowed your workflow by shifting from one platform to another, find the buried gold and sell the benefits to your team. For example, we once typed on manual typewriters. Then we started using word processors, typing into a little window and hitting "Enter" when a document was ready to be printed. After that, we had WordPerfect for DOS, then Word-Perfect for Windows, and then Microsoft Word. Before long, Word was the world's number-one word-processing program. Did you resent the inconveniences of learning a new system as you progressed from one to the other? Perhaps it was irritating at the time, but,

looking back, it's easy to see how the changes benefited you in the end.

2. *Reframe the challenge as an opportunity.* Rather than worry about the difficulty you'll face as a result of the change, offer it as a benefit: a chance to learn something new, improve your workflow, and increase your mental flexibility. It's especially effective if you can see change as an adventure. Accept the possibility that the change may prove good for you, if you let it. Many people initially resisted remote "cloud" backup for their files because they didn't understand it. They were afraid they'd lose data if they tried services like Mozy or CrashPlan. Yet it's clearly the wave of the future, and most who have faced the challenge squarely have found it not only easy but fascinating. This resource opens whole new possibilities for enhanced productivity.

3. *Phase it in gradually.* With rare exceptions, you don't have to dump your old way of doing something in favor of the new right away. Generally, you'll have time to thoroughly investigate the change, dig up and distribute the gold nuggets, and provide any necessary training or tools to smooth the transition.

These three tactics represent only a few ways of embracing change. Don't change just for the sake of change; you don't have to. Change will inevitably find you.

GOOD ENOUGH NEVER IS

Knowing when to institute change requires a shrewd mind and keen insight. But at the end of the day, it boils down to something this basic: a desire to always get better.

Conservatism has its place, but business requires calculated risk. You and your team must be willing to try the new and different to improve your results and skyrocket your productivity. In fact, to stay in the lead, you'll have to continuously improve. Keep these tips in mind:

1. *Act on change.* In the business arena, nothing stays the same for long. It makes no sense to pick one strategy and stick with it forever. Your processes must evolve along with marketplace conditions and technology.

2. *Teamwork rules.* You can't drag people into the future. Encourage personal improvement, demand excellence, and ensure everyone believes in and takes teamwork seriously. Constantly refined and consistently applied, teamwork offers the best opportunity for aligning with the organization's goals and strategies. Never let anyone settle for "good enough."

3. *Test and tweak.* Keep an eye on your processes and systems, making sure they flex along with the changes. Occasionally test various aspects of your workflow to see if you can make them function even better. Sometimes even a slight change can make a big difference. But take care to change only one thing at a time, so you can identify what generates the improvement.

4. *Organize everything.* Everything must have its place and needs to stay in that place when not in use. Clean up the clutter and institute intuitive filing systems, so you can locate data in a minute or less. Document each process to allow new team members to get up to speed.

5. *Push the envelope.* Always try to exceed your previous score. That's how Olympic athletes break records and top-notch employees continue to dominate their pro-

fessions. "Good enough" hurts you, because it eventually softens into complacency, and then backslides into mediocrity. With an ever-increasing baseline for status quo, standing still inevitably means falling behind.

6. *Embrace change yourself.* You may be tired of gurus telling you to "lead by example," but it's crucial. If you're stuck in the past, why should your team bother to try anything new? Become an early adopter of technology and processes alike. That way, you can discover what works best and offer pointers to those who follow.

7. *Be open to suggestions.* Encourage your team members to open their minds to the idea of improvement through change, so they can evolve to better fit their environment. Then make it easy for them to make suggestions on how to do so.

8. *Identify and motivate change leaders.* Genuine enthusiasm is infectious, and those who have it stand out like supernovas. So give incentives to employees who honestly appreciate the improvements that well-applied change can bring. Change leaders not only push fellow employees to greater heights but also attract more change leaders.

9. *Get out of the way.* Once you've urged your people to accept the concept of continuous improvement, get out of their way and let them make changes. When they know they can own their jobs, work becomes more than a way to earn a living—they put pieces of their souls into it and take it to the limit.

10. *Celebrate improvement.* When your team improves its productivity and profitability through change, throw a party. Nothing succeeds like success, and, if you're

careful not to rest on your laurels, you can build on positive change to create more. It's like the penny in the children's song "Magic Penny"; it multiplies the more you lend and spend it.

Any organization that fails to practice continuous improvement sabotages itself in the long run. So keep your eyes open and keep stretching your boundaries.

SPARK INNOVATIVE THINKING

Remember Peter Drucker's rule: "The business enterprise has two—and only two—basic functions: marketing and innovation."

Ironically, we encourage maturity in our kids as they grow up. Generally, that requires them to shut down their innate creativity. Then what happens? Many jobs require creativity to maximize productivity and profit. Without creativity, we can't innovate.

While the business environment requires a certain level of built-in routine to function, that doesn't mean you can't have creative fun at work. So throw open the floodgates in your own mind and encourage your people to do the same. Let's look at a few ways you can increase innovation in your organization.

1. *Foster an open, creative work environment.*
   To foster creativity, some companies provide workers with snacks, games, and "time off" during work hours. Encourage communication, a positive attitude, and a low-stress environment. All these support the mental flexibility and unshackled thought processes that result in innovation.

2. *Motivate your team.* Positive reinforcement in the form of rewards, bonuses, special privileges, comp

time, and prizes will keep people on their toes. Not everyone will participate, but many will when they see their efforts result in clear benefits.

3. *Encourage diversity.* A wide range of working styles, thought processes, and viewpoints is essential to come up with a wide range of creative solutions. Innovation grows only in a well-fertilized field. Rather than stunt its growth, find ways to encourage interaction. Brainstorm with your team, bring in outsiders occasionally for their perspectives, and cross-fertilize your ideas with other teams.

4. *Don't penalize.* If your team members fear punishment if their initiatives fail, why should they even try? Becoming innovative requires risking failure. That's part of the creative mindset, because you'll fail more often than you'll succeed. Consider providing a suggestion box, so employees can contribute anonymously. Even in an open environment, some people prefer confidentiality.

To encourage innovation, make it a part of your basic workflow process. You can do as Combe does and force a certain level of innovation. That may sound contradictory, but this approach seems to work. John Alberto told me,

> In our business, the biggest spend we have is on advertising, which is the same for any consumer company—Procter & Gamble, Johnson & Johnson, Colgate, and so on. As the CEO, you should be demanding that when people come back with their marketing plans, a certain percentage of their dollars spent on marketing be on things that they have never spent the money on before, to force innovation—even if you don't know if it will succeed. Have people come back, be it every six months or once a year, and ask them, "Ten percent

of your money was to be spent on stuff you've never spent it on before. What did you spend it on, and what did you learn?"

This is being done at the best consumer companies in the world. They're driving innovation on purpose—even if it means failing forward fast—because of the learning, and sharing that learning, whether it's successful or not. Even in the process of doing that, I'm sure the discovery of what does work will be organic in many cases, which is the whole nature of efficient execution. And you can still build on the things that don't work. You might have the right idea, but the wrong execution; but then you can build on that.

SWING FOR THE BLEACHERS

According to a BlessingWhite study in 2007, most managers don't encourage risk-taking.[5] Only 26 percent of the employees surveyed were ever encouraged by their employers to look for new solutions or take risks. Yet business requires calculated risk and innovation.

Further, only 50 percent of those who took risks received praise when those risks panned out; 35 percent were ignored; and 9 percent were criticized. Clearly there's double-talk going on—that is, many managers say they want to see initiative and innovation, but they don't want to deal with the fallout when something new doesn't work. They worry more about toeing the line and meeting constant pressure to deliver immediate results.

If you desire innovation, you must be serious about what you expect of your employees. Revamp your attitude so you can handle more flexibility yourself. Emphasize that it's okay to make mistakes, unless it causes severe damage to the organization or its reputation. And naturally, you can't tolerate consistent failure or complacency.

Once you've done all this, step back and let 'em go. You'll soon see results, especially in their self-motivation, self-confidence, greater organizational loyalty, and increased interest in learning.

BOUNCE BACK QUICKLY

Develop a high level of internal flexibility in your team, group, division, or department, so you can accommodate whatever the world throws at you—predictable or not. Among other things, flexibility helps your organization detect and cash in on emerging trends, providing better service as client needs and desires evolve.

Flexibility does require fast response, but it also allows you to maximize your freedom of movement even while working within the constraints of corporate and governmental rules. If that sounds contradictory, it needn't be. Consider the sonnet, a poetic form that requires the poet to work within specific constraints regarding length, rhythm, and rhyme scheme. The structure is rigid, but the poet has plenty of freedom within that structure—in fact, the rules may ultimately force greater creativity and better performance. The same holds true for organizations.

But what happens when an organization is so rigid that it breaks rather than bends when the winds of change blow? You end up with sad failures like Hostess Brands, terminally bankrupt after more than eighty years in business. Sadly, Hostess's leaders weren't flexible enough as times changed. They failed to accommodate customer demands for healthier snacks as junk food became less popular. The company's production costs rose and its income stream crashed.

Hostess leadership apparently didn't learn from a previous failure in the 1980s, when it went bankrupt the first time. Perhaps the third time's the charm. As of this writing, Hostess Brands has come back under new owners as a leaner operation without union employees, retail stores, or the vast pile of debt its previous incarnation had accumulated.

Prediction and Preparation

Although flexible organizations tend to focus on foreseeable changes, the best systems can handle the unpredictable as well. They typically do so through rule modeling, the establishment of decision-making schemes that allow those with the proper authority to handle any situation. Rule modeling's opposite number, sequential planning, demands a solution for every potential problem. It also enforces a rigid, stepwise decision-making process in unvarying sequence. While this system is absolutely necessary for some professions like piloting, it hobbles everyone else.

It's time to ask: What's the worst thing that could happen to our organization right now? Consider contingency plans for likely possibilities, so you can take advantage of new situations as they arise. Business goals can shift or evolve at any time, in any direction.

Be prepared to respond to anything, not just predictable events like regulatory changes, evolving customer demands, legal challenges, and competitive threats. You also have to be able to handle the unexpected, like abrupt changes in partner/supply networks; the firing, transfer, or resignation of crucial team members; natural disasters; illnesses; deaths; war; criminal acts; terrorism; and giant exploding meteors. If that last one sounds a bit silly, Google what happened on February 15, 2013, in the city of Chelyabinsk, Russia.

Not everything unexpected is as physically destructive as the items listed, but even cultural shifts can be devastating. For example, suppose you've pinned your entire business on manufacturing a single type of product. What happens if that product suddenly becomes useless or unpopular? When everyone was carrying a laptop, do you suppose many laptop manufacturers asked, "What would happen if people stopped using laptops?" Well, at least one did. Apple's iPad refined the tablet computer industry, and suddenly laptops weren't as necessary as they used to be. The other manufacturers struggled to catch up. Then Amazon, already known for its nifty Kindle e-readers, released the Kindle Fire for less than $200. Have we seen the end of laptops, especially now that we can store our data in the cloud and access it anywhere?

In another example of an industry blindsided by change (though it shouldn't have been), newspapers have yet to recover from the development of the Internet, much less their new availability on paperless technology. Their leaders should have had a crisis plan in place for something unforeseeable—or at least have had the wisdom to look outside their narrow box. They did not.

Developing built-in flexibility may sound challenging, but it doesn't necessarily require increased complexity. Your best bet is to build robust systems that cover a wide range of possibilities. Make sure you've based those systems on a multidisciplinary approach with constant awareness of prevailing business conditions and minimum lag time between stimulus and response.

If you plan ways to bounce back no matter how badly change impacts you, then, like one of those inflatable clown punching bags, nothing can keep you down for long.

Resilience and Expansion

Positive or negative, change can bring damage with it. Even when everything goes right, an organization can suffer from growing pains as it overextends itself. It may even end up smaller than it was when it started out.

Consider what happened to the British Empire when it grew too large. Its leaders got so busy handling a few territories at the expense of others that revolution and decay set in. That's one reason the United States of America is an independent country today.

Continued success relies on robustness and resilience for survival, whether you've been smashed flat or overinflated. Every time you run into something new, learn from it so it won't catch you off guard again. Bureaucracy represents the enemy here, because no bureaucracy in the world is capable of doing in one minute what it can do in ten. Instead, establish fluid rule modeling, with flexible structures to support both what's happening today and any emergent competitive advantages you may encounter.

That said, also establish system constraints to fight randomness and anarchy. They need not be complex: shared mission/vision statements, motivation/reward systems, and mobilization plans can be relatively easy to implement (if you haven't already). Add these to your basic strategies and build an organizational framework to handle the unexpected. Then you'll have an excellent recipe for resilience.

Implementing such strategies when you don't have to almost always backfires. The roster of failed organizations that forgot (or ignored) this reality is too numerous to list. But ask yourself: Where are electronics retailers Circuit City and clothiers Steve & Barry's today?

Consistency lets you rebound when conditions let up, whereas cutbacks don't. So rather than chew off something important in an attempt to escape the business trap you've put yourself in, find a way to pry open the trap instead. Keep your mind alert to the possibilities, be creative, and ask: "What must we do to make it happen?"

Saying, "It can't be done" should be a firing offense. Five thousand years ago, people with no modern technology built the equivalent of skyscrapers with log rollers, levers, ramps, and hard work. People walked on the moon more than forty years ago using the primitive aerospace and computer technology of the day. Given what we have now, who knows what we can (and can't) do when sufficiently challenged?

Mother Nature and human nature both operate on the basic rule of "adapt or die." Your long-term survival may well depend on your resilience and the ability to zig when the rest of the world zags. That's the essence of flexibility. If you've managed to stay more or less whole by the time you've worked your way clear of your troubles, the sky's the limit.

Not only can you bounce back, but you can also bounce back beyond your original boundaries—and keep growing to replace others who have fallen by the wayside.

Reorganize Quickly

Most of the successful companies I work with are constantly reorganizing as the business environment changes. You can't stay in one place for long, or your structure won't reflect the reality of modern business. As Cisco's Debbie Gross pointed out,

> You have to be able to adapt to change, be flexible to change, accept change, and embrace change. The companies that don't do that tend to fall behind. Take, for example, Hewlett-Packard—a behemoth of a company that did a great job with printers and PCs but may have tried to change a little too late.
>
> HP was in a low-margin commodity business, got too fat, and couldn't move quickly enough. It had leaders who went in and made some poor acquisitions, trying to catch up with the market. You have to catch the market trends when they're happening, because if you wait too long, they just pass you by. Then it's too late to catch up.

CRASH THROUGH THE FEAR BARRIER

What are the three most significant events in aviation history?

Well, in 1903, the Wright brothers made their maiden flight, which launched the world of aviation. In 1969, the Apollo 11 moon landing took place. Those two are easy. But what was the third significant event in the sixty-six years between? Most aviation historians believe it happened on October 14, 1954, when Chuck Yeager entered his Bell X-1 rocket airplane for the ninth time. He was airlifted by a B-29 to a great height and then dropped. He experienced free-fall for about 500 feet. Then he fired his rockets.

Yeager took his plane to 42,000 feet, accelerated to a speed of 768 miles per hour, and sustained that speed for 20 seconds, breaking the sound barrier. Until he did so, most people thought the sound barrier couldn't be broken without destroying the aircraft. Others had found that, when approaching that barrier, their aircraft vibrated violently. That day, Chuck Yeager found that after he exceeded the speed of sound, the violent shaking ended, and the ride was as smooth as glass.

Change won't be as hard as you think. It's scary as you're going through it, but once you break your personal sound barrier—the fears in your own life—you might discover that it's smooth sailing on the other side.

THE FINAL WORD

We live in a dynamic world. A line graph tracking change in the last few centuries manifests as a steep parabolic curve with no end in sight—and the billions of vibrant personalities that compose humanity make it all the more chaotic.

What doesn't grow either stagnates or rots. So, knowing that change is necessary, keep working to better your team.

Make incremental improvements when possible, and take quantum leaps when necessary.

Some of the world's oldest companies started out doing completely different things than they do now. The Hudson's Bay Company no longer dominates the Northeast fur trade any more than Oneida still makes bear traps, but that's how those companies got started. They still exist because they're willing to adapt as circumstances warrant.

Some organizations take too long to move a product to market. For example, when W. L. Gore & Associates developed Glide Floss, the medical-technology group at Gore objected to marketing it for twenty years after its invention! The company manufactured sophisticated vascular grafts and heart valves, so its leaders were concerned that putting the Gore name on dental floss would hurt the company's image as a medical-technology leader.

John Spencer joined the company in 1991, heard about the languished product, and got excited. He used clinical trials to validate the product, proving people preferred Glide Floss over other brands hands-down. Then he started a grassroots marketing campaign and persuaded Happy Harry's, a Delaware drugstore chain, to stock Glide in twenty-six stores. He gave samples to dentists and said if their customers liked it, they could buy more at Happy Harry's. His goal was to sell 600 units in the first three months. Customers snapped up 12,000 units and clamored for more. Glide even became part of a *Seinfeld* TV episode. Within eighteen months, it became the best-selling dental floss in the United States.

You'll either be a bright light shining through the decades or a forgotten blip on the radar screen of history. Roll with change as it inevitably occurs. Like the dinosaurs, you'll die if you can't evolve.

Ensure Engaged, Empowered Employees

You've surely noticed that when you have more at stake and are more interested in your work, you're more likely to do a better job (or at least try to).

Your team members feel the same way. Why should they spend their precious discretionary effort on the strategic goals you set when they don't enjoy their jobs? That's especially true if they aren't encouraged or allowed to take the initiative to improve conditions or make those last-minute changes vital to timely strategic execution.

Wouldn't you rather be surrounded by people who love their work and trust you to let them get on with their jobs without undue interference? In this chapter, I'll show you some simple, common-sense ways to achieve that confident competence.

THE MIRACLE OF ENGAGEMENT

While you might be tempted at times, you can't simply fire all the underperformers on your team, or you might not have much of a team left. A more effective solution is to encourage employee engagement—which, unless you've been living under a rock, you've heard a lot about lately.

Engagement is critical for execution, because studies have repeatedly shown that engaged employees are more productive. Simply put, the higher the percentage of engagement, the greater the success of any company, large or small.

An engaged employee is one who's enthusiastic and fully involved with his or her job and organization. That person sincerely contributes to both team and organizational success. Engaged employees have pride in what they do for a living and feel proud about where they work.

Employee engagement studies typically split employees into three categories: the actively engaged, the unengaged, and the actively disengaged. Depending on the study cited, somewhere between 17 and 29 percent of employees are actively engaged. About half are unengaged. These people like their jobs and may be good at them, but they don't care much about the company's strategic goals. At the bottom of the heap are the rest—the 17 to 29 percent who are actively disengaged. These uncommitted people go to work only to get their paychecks. They couldn't give two hoots about the company's mission and vision, even if they knew what they were. They're just marking time until retirement.[6]

Fortunately, it's possible for you as a leader to change those numbers—and crucial that you try. Time and again, researchers have found that the relationship between employee and manager offers an excellent gauge of the employee's engagement level. That's because workers don't leave companies; they leave managers.

If that sounds as though it's all on your shoulders, well, to a large extent it is. To most employees, you're the direct representative of the company and possibly the only such representative they encounter regularly.

Engaged employees are the type of people you build an organization around; they're the ones you count on to help take your organization to the next level. According to a recent study by Gallup Consulting (the famous pollsters), world-class businesses have ratios of engaged employees to disengaged employees of about 9.57:1, as opposed to only 1.83:1 for average businesses. Gallup sets an engaged:disengaged benchmark of 8:1 for successful, world-class companies, thus providing a standard to shoot for.[7]

The researchers noted that actively disengaged workers cost American companies an estimated $300 billion annually in lost productivity. In 2003, Towers Perrin–ISR found that companies with high levels of engagement saw their operating profits rise by an average of 3.74 percent over three years, while those with low levels of engagement showed drops in net profits and operating margins on the order of 1.38 percent and 2.01 percent, respectively.[8] And consider the fact that, in the long run, engaged companies outperform their less-engaged competitors by up to 28 percent (one of the key findings of the Conference Board study of 2006).[9]

The Q12 Calculation

To determine the level of engagement, Gallup offers a Q12 employee engagement survey—that is, twelve questions it asks every employee when addressing the topic. Some of the questions may seem odd, but together they identify what Gallup calls "strong feelings of employee engagement."[10]

Basically, Gallup asks the following:

1. Do you know what is expected of you at work?

2. Do you have the materials and equipment you need to do your work right?

3. At work, do you have the opportunity to do what you do best every day?

4. In the last seven days, have you received recognition or praise for doing good work?

5. Does your supervisor, or someone at work, seem to care about you as a person?

6. Is there someone at work who encourages your development?

7. At work, do your opinions seem to count?

8. Does the mission/purpose of your company make you feel your job is important?

9. Are your associates (fellow employees) committed to doing quality work?

10. Do you have a best friend at work?

11. In the last six months, has someone at work talked to you about your progress?

12. In the last year, have you had opportunities at work to learn and grow?

Individual responses should make it fairly easy to determine what you need to work on to maximize employee engagement within your team. Of course, you'll never get everyone engaged; there will always be that occasional sourpuss you can't reach. But if you can meet or exceed Gallup's 8:1 benchmark, your team will outshine nearly all your competitors.

Putting Engagement into Drive

"Chick-fil-A has been very blessed to have a highly engaged workforce, relative to other organizations, as demonstrated by our high scores on the Q12," Roger Blythe told me.

> We have a very strong sense of culture and corporate purpose, so the people we end up attracting to the organization, for the most part, resonate with that. Our business has also been very blessed financially, so we haven't really had a sudden change of direction, layoffs, or a big intervention that can create cultural confusion. We're privately owned, so we don't have a new CEO every three to five years setting out in new directions.

Clearly, shared purpose is key in achieving and sustaining outstanding productivity, if only because it has the potential to increase employee retention. Engaged employees are far more productive and valuable than average workers or the actively disengaged. Naturally, this driver affects the bottom line, so doing everything you can to increase employee engagement is simply good business. That requires understanding what factors drive engagement and knowing how you can implement them.

Several interrelated factors drive engagement, including (but not limited to) the following:

- Confidence in one's ability to do the job properly.

- Having control over work with minimal oversight.

- The nature and quality of the job itself.

- Access to training and career development.

- Opportunities for growth.

- Ongoing communication and feedback from

management, especially when conveying information and congratulating good work.

- A clear understanding of the company's goals and why employee contributions matter.

- Pride in the company and your place in it.

- Opportunities to work in a team environment.

- Relationships with team members and other coworkers.

- Trust in the company and its integrity.

- Presence of a confident, competent, and supportive manager.

The bullet point on trust is especially important. According to recent surveys, only about half of American workers trust the people at the top of their companies' organizational charts.[11] However, about three-quarters of workers trust their immediate managers (including 51 percent of the disengaged ones).[12]

That's good, because trust is a critical factor in creating and maintaining engagement—a big part of your success as leader.

BE THERE OR BE SQUARE

To create an environment in which people can execute quickly and are willing to do so, be sure to provide multiple mechanisms for team members to get feedback, give feedback, give status updates, and get course corrections. It's a continual communication process, not a once-a-year performance review. That requires you to spend a lot of time being hands-on with your people, while keeping them connected to team and organizational priorities. As Mike Howard of Microsoft told me,

> When you have a vision, you have to get it out to the people to the point where they get tired of hearing about it. Then it's part of their DNA. To me, this is done in the interface with people. My job is strategic vision, leadership, and touch points with my team, not tactics. I make myself available to them. Once a week, I go to our other buildings and work there for at least a half-day, so the folks there can get some face time. I'll walk around and have no set agenda but just talk to people and see how they're doing. It's a big part of creating an environment where people feel engaged. More than anything, it's about engagement with the leaders.

If you have the resources, you can implement a strategy of one-on-one weekly meetings with key employees, ensuring face-time with everyone to guarantee they "get it" on a strategic level. If once a week won't work, attempt a once-monthly meeting with each person on your team. The meetings need not be long; you simply want to help employees understand how their execution of the strategy—and their willingness to take the organization's future into their hands in the moment—is crucial to its long-term success.

Yes, occasionally their decisions may prove wrong; that's the risky nature of business. But as computer pioneer Rear Admiral Grace Hopper once pointed out (and my father the Air Force colonel loved to repeat), it's easier to ask forgiveness than to get permission. This is especially true in modern business, when there's often no time to go through the permission process.

Management by Walking Around

Back in 1939, two electronics pioneers named Bill Hewlett and Dave Packard founded a company that (after a coin-toss) they named Hewlett-Packard. Now famous among the public for its top-notch computer equipment, Hewlett-Packard enjoys nearly as much fame in business circles for its open management style—the so-called HP Way. This method includes a surprisingly simple element called MBWA, short for management by walking around.

The name describes the process. Rather than spending all of their time closeted in an office, managers occasionally wander around the workplace visiting with individual workers and talking with them about their work-related concerns. This encourages a closer relationship with the workforce and helps each manager find ways to increase workplace productivity.

In their 1982 book *In Search of Excellence,* Tom Peters and Robert Waterman gave this management method a boost when they identified it as a common practice among the world's best-run companies.[13]

MBWA has a lot going for it, because it helps you stay connected with your team members, thus letting them know you care about them and what they think. It fits well with the "open door" management philosophy, though both can be taken too far if they eat into your personal productivity. And if you become too enthusiastic about MBWA, you tread perilously close to micromanagement. So avoid standing around telling people exactly what to do; instead, chat with them openly and uncritically, have fun, watch and listen, and possibly try doing their work for a bit.

How you handle the details and intensity of your MBWA rounds is up to you. While most managers set aside a few hours for it (a reasonable time frame), some go all out. According to some reports, the late Steve Jobs sometimes took technical support phone calls at Apple. Similarly, Abraham Lincoln inspected randomly chosen Union Army units early in the Civil War.

Given the time investment required, I don't recommend

the Jobs/Lincoln approach. But do give MBWA some thought and see if you can fit it into your management style. Done well, MBWA can:

- Motivate people when you talk to them one-on-one.

- Make you seem more sympathetic and less isolated from their concerns than might otherwise be the case.

- Show your people you care about more than the company's bottom line; you care about them.

THAT OTHER SCARY E-WORD: EMPOWERMENT

In the high-octane world of modern business, you hear plenty of theories about what it takes to increase employee productivity. In addition to engagement, the concept of empowerment is mentioned quite often, especially as it relates to the corporate team environment.

The concept is simple enough: when you implement practices that help employees feel confident, capable, and in control of the outcome of their work, they are empowered to do that work effectively. Ideally, this ensures commitment to the company's core mission, vision, and values, resulting in greater productivity over the long term.

That's the theory, anyway. But, as any scientist will tell you, all that matters is how well a theory stands up to testing. If it's a dud, a few experimental runs in the real world will soon put that theory to rest.

So how does the employee empowerment schema fare? It works like gangbusters. Real-world testing has repeatedly proven that the best employees are those who own their work: that is, those who believe they have a say in how they do their work while being fully engaged in both the process and outcome.

Empowered employees aren't just proud of their work; they're more productive than their disempowered colleagues. They're also more satisfied, so they bring in more business by making customers happy, which translates into higher profits. From a hard-nosed financial perspective, employee empowerment totally makes sense.

But even when they're willing to consider the strategy, leaders often develop a false idea of what empowerment means. As a result, they shoot themselves in the metaphorical foot when they try to implement it. So before exploring what you can do to implement employee empowerment, let's look at what empowerment is not. For starters:

- Empowerment isn't a right; it's a privilege. Individuals should be fully empowered by management only when they prove they can do the job and display the proper initiative. On the other hand, the *opportunity* to become empowered should be a right.

- Employees don't always automatically assume empowerment, no matter what management may think. If your employees aren't taking the initiative to own their jobs, they don't feel empowered to do so, possibly because you haven't made it clear that they can.

- Empowerment isn't a bunch of motivational posters or empty slogans to which management pays lip service but doesn't follow.

- Empowerment isn't a blank check for anything the employee wants. Management must set explicit boundaries within a strategic framework. That way, employees will know and understand which decisions they can make without management approval.

- Empowerment isn't management by consensus. Rather, when properly implemented, it gives workers the authority to do their own jobs, not the work of the management.

Employee empowerment boils down to a philosophy that allows employees to think for themselves within definite but broad limits. Some observers claim that empowerment comes from the employee, and to a certain extent that's true. However, I submit that true workplace empowerment comes from employees and management working in tandem. As with engagement, employees must be willing to show initiative and take control of their work. However, leaders must be in a position to both allow and encourage empowerment, or it will never occur.

Which brings me to this crucial point: Management has a regrettable tendency to express a commitment to empowerment without actually making it an effective part of the environment.

No doubt you've seen productivity initiatives fizzle. Management somehow got the impression that a few catchy slogans and a coffee mug (or worse, something silly like an "empowerment rock") would actually empower employees to buy into the organization's mission and vision and take ownership of their work. It's hard to say why companies waste resources this way. I suspect it stems from an unwillingness to relinquish control to the employees, or from a fear of losing certain privileges.

Whatever the case, as a leader, if you're wishy-washy about empowerment, you're unlikely to see a significant productivity increase when you try to implement it. Even in these uncertain times, the most you'll see is employees who do only what they must to get by. Never underestimate your team members. They're keenly aware of what you think of them, and a halfhearted effort at empowerment will go over like a lead balloon.

The irony is that employee empowerment isn't all that difficult or expensive to implement.

Engaging the Engine of Empowerment

Direct involvement and supportive communication on the part of management make up the two pillars of employee empowerment.

First, you have to make your employees understand what you want to achieve. You can't do so simply by ordering them to do this or that without explaining why. Employees aren't soldiers. They haven't been through the intensive training the military uses to break down individuals and rebuild them into the type of fighters it requires.

So help your employees understand what your team needs to accomplish. Explain the organization's mission in a straightforward way. It can be as simple as, "We're trying to make the best tires in the world," or "We're world leaders in software technology, and we want to stay that way." You don't have to ramble or use buzz phrases about "leveraging our core business" and "optimizing quality-driven geo-targeted bandwidth," or "performing gap analysis," even though all that may be integral to your business strategy. Give it to them straight.

Give of Yourself

Speaking of giving, effective leaders must also be willing to give of themselves. Treat employees the way you want people to treat you. You should:

- Provide assistance appropriate to the problems employees face.

- Help when requested and when doing so is reasonable.

- Provide information or express concern in a way that neither embarrasses people nor causes them to lose face (hence the saying, "Praise in public, criticize in private").

Let's be clear on this: Empowering employees to do their jobs confidently and without excessive oversight does not represent a purely altruistic move (although your employees may think so). When properly handled, employee empowerment is a win-win situation all around, because in addition to making employees more productive, it also makes *you* more productive. By tapping into the knowledge and energy of your employees, you not only take advantage of the "many heads are better than one" thesis, but you also get to focus on your own most profitable tasks.

At your level, tasks like marketing, coaching, inventing, and hiring top-notch employees become a whole lot more profitable than putting out brush fires or doing menial tasks. Planning a marketing blitz that could bring in a million bucks is far more productive than helping your intern photocopy a report.

MONEY . . . IT'S A HIT

I believe you're always better off using a carrot rather than a stick on your employees. If you really want your team members to feel empowered, reward them for their productivity or otherwise tell them you appreciate their contributions.

Extrinsic rewards can involve ways to celebrate success: have a party, deliver a cheesecake to the break room, or go out for a team lunch. Sure, celebrations cost a bit, but they represent a good investment that can boost morale, enhance output, and reduce stress. I send my office manager Becca to a pedicure after an especially crazy deadline. You could try prizes, bonuses, handing out T-shirts, hats, and mugs to commemorate a success, days off, and free vacations—whatever your imagination can conceive.

Money is always a popular reward. In addition to pay raises based on meeting certain milestones, rewards can include the proceeds of quality contests (e.g., those who find new ways to maximize production receive special bonuses) as well as one-time bonuses for delivering the goods on time and under budget.

You don't always have to offer people money to stimulate their interest in being more agile and productive. While many people love trophies, gift cards, and the like, for some, less obvious intrinsic awards can be equally as powerful as extrinsic ones.

One example of an intrinsic award is asking accomplished personnel to take on other important assignments (though this comes dangerously close to the practice of "the better you do, the more work you get," which can drive workers to burnout). Other possibilities include allowing the team to meet off-site rather than in the office. A verbal "pat on the back" will suffice for some, and a simple acknowledgment in the company newsletter can add a little shine to their lives. Even better is sending a letter to your CEO lauding their efforts. Thank-you notes, title changes, special parking spaces, and prime office locations can also inspire employees to greater heights.

Even more important, the rewards must apply to everyone equally. There can be no favoritism or even the appearance of favoritism. Those who meet the criteria for a reward or recognition should receive it automatically and as soon after the high-performance action as possible. That will reinforce the type of behavior you want to see in them and others.

THE FINAL WORD

Increasing your ratio of engaged employees can be hard work. The task requires not only strength but flexibility and empathy. Yes, this can take a lot of work on your part, but if you end up with competent employees who make you and your organization shine, it'll be worth every bit of effort.

Ultimately, employees work hard because they choose to. Anyone with more than a few months of experience in a position knows where the line marking "good enough" lies. If people lack any reason to do otherwise, most will park themselves just this side of sufficient. They may not be lazy, but until you give them an incentive, why should they work any harder than they have to?

Therefore, one aspect of your job is to encourage your people to spend their discretionary effort on the team. That can take a wide variety of forms, from empowerment and engagement efforts to monetary rewards, time off, praise, and your personal involvement. Make consistent efforts to influence team members in positive ways, varying your efforts to see what works best.

If you can persuade them to give you more of their discretionary effort, productivity will skyrocket—and you'll be walking on sunshine.

KEY

Alignment

ALIGNMENT

Leadership Role
Conductor: Steer It

*Development
Opportunity*
Communication/
Productivity

Like a conductor of a symphony, today's leader is out front watching what's going on, keeping everyone on the right track, steering team members toward the organization's strategic priorities, and listening to their best ideas on how to get there.

Alignment means your strategic priorities and the day-to-day operations of your team are synchronized. Their tactics are carrying out your strategies.

The old "command and control" structure no longer works. As I pointed out in my recent book, *What to Do When There's Too Much to Do*,[14] there's a constant

121

pressure in the business world to do more and become more productive, creating a rush to cram even more work into the limited time we have and the minutes we save.

Ironically, the only way to accomplish more is to do less. That is, to cut back on less productive and less profitable activities in favor of what matters most and achieves a greater result. In this book, I elevate this central concept to the leadership level. All people who are successful, innovative, and creative want to do more and more. But on that route lies strain, fatigue, burnout, family issues, and even death (as expressed in the Japanese concept of *karoshi*).

As leader, you have to take a hand in helping your team members harness their overachiever tendencies in a positive way, so you can maximize productivity and maintain it at a reasonable level. While you'll always have to work hard, it's best to focus on the outcome, which must align tightly with overarching organizational goals as well as your team's goals.

To accomplish this, pick only a small number of goals to work on at a time—or the law of diminishing returns will come into play. Your people already have their regular daily activities to handle. If you add too much to their plate, they may feel defeated and give up, so work within the limits set by reality. Better to hit three goals solidly than twenty halfway. Have you heard Voltaire's classic adage, "The perfect is the enemy of the good"? Trying to do too many things too well often results in the paralysis of analysis, a sort of mental vapor lock in which you accomplish nothing significant.

Remember, whenever you say "yes" to something, you have to say "no" to something else. Realizing that, help your team focus their finite energy and time on activities that will support your strategic priorities. This may involve setting reasonable limits and ending one failing project to make room for a better one.

As a leader, how can you accomplish this? Begin by helping your people internalize the rules of alignment based on thoroughly knowing the goals themselves. It's the day-to-day action that moves the needle, so make sure that what your team is doing right now will get you to where you need to be.

Specifically, your team members need to know:

- *Why should they care?* Why is the mission important and compelling to them?

- *What is the goal?* What are they expected to achieve, so they know when they've arrived?

- *How do we get there?* Who's responsible for what? What's the timeline for completion? How will you measure milestones and otherwise keep track of progress? What will other team members do to help? What rewards (intrinsic or extrinsic) will they receive? How will you hold them accountable for the desired results?

In this part of the book, we'll look at answers to those key questions.

Take Your Team on a Mission

Besides collecting a paycheck, what is an employee's motivation for achieving a particular strategic goal? Why should they care?

At my Uncle David's wedding several years ago, I had a profound conversation with a close family friend named Brian. Brian was David's neighbor and his best man. Because of bad weather in Chicago (no surprise), he'd had major flight delays and other problems getting back to his home in San Antonio for the rehearsal dinner. He got there just in time to run into the church and take his place. Later at the dinner, I was thinking about the stress he certainly experienced and told him, "I heard about all the craziness with your travel yesterday. I'm so sorry."

"Oh, the flight was fine," he replied. "I'm just delighted to be here."

"What a drag!" I rambled. "Weather can be so frustrating. Several years ago, we had a huge blizzard in Denver, and it stranded people right at Christmas!"

"Oh, you know, it actually doesn't bother me. I didn't have an agenda. I had a *mission*."

Brian's statement immediately struck me as insightful, and has stayed with me since. Why not make achieving your organization's goals a mission? Your ability to clearly articulate your strategic priorities depends on understanding why you're here and what you're trying to accomplish.

Think of pilots sometimes flying by their instruments in inclement weather, or military organizations "painting" their targets with radar to achieve hits at night. You have to know what your target is to hit it consistently. You might not always be able to see the target, but you must be able to visualize it and paint the picture for others.

As a leader, communicating your mission involves conveying why you care and why others should also care. So invite your employees to go on a mission with you. Help them understand why your organization's priorities are important, whether at the team, department, division, or company level.

Get Your Ducks in a Row

One of the business world's basic realities is that organizational strategy doesn't always align well with day-to-day operations—that is, the short-term tactics and logistics that combine to ensure the organization stays afloat. Indeed, bringing the two together may represent the most difficult part of your job.

It's tough at any level, especially on the front lines where workers have a hard enough time taking care of their basic duties, plus all the new stuff their bosses throw at them. But then, organizational strategy probably doesn't get much mention in their job descriptions. I'll bet it does in yours, though. As a leader, you get paid the big bucks to align overall goals with the daily slog . . . because what's the point of the slog if it goes nowhere?

I take it as an article of faith—and I trust you do, too—

that people do better work when they can engage with and own their jobs. Conversely, they won't care much if they believe their work doesn't matter. So do your very best to show them how it does. I recommend the 3-T Method: Tell, Teach, and Train. Each step intertwines with the others at a basic level.

1. *Tell.* Don't expect most employees to go out of their way to dig up the company's mission and vision statements. They just don't have the time. Instead, meet with each one and tell them exactly why their daily work matters and how it fits into the organization's overall strategy. Once they realize they matter (and especially that the higher-ups know they do), they'll be more likely to take ownership of their work, show initiative, unleash their creativity, and do a better job all around.

2. *Teach.* Once you've shown your people how and why they matter, carry it forward by empowering them. As the work situation or industry evolves, keep them in the loop. Post metrics to demonstrate how their work has gotten everyone closer to the finish line. Mentor them, helping them to grow into and beyond their jobs so they can step into positions of greater responsibility—and honestly offer them a realistic chance of advancement. Nothing kills engagement like realizing you're in a dead-end job.

3. *Train.* Consistently educate your team members in new procedures, software applications, and additions to their job descriptions. Don't hesitate to help them refine their existing skills. Just because you have one type of hammer, for example, doesn't mean you can use it for all hammering tasks. Ever try to hang a picture using a sledgehammer?

Facing the Future

Depending on your situation, you may not find the 3-Ts easy to implement. But the concept itself is simple enough. Think of each step as an investment, because in the long run, the process will save you money. You'll find it cheaper to Tell, Teach, and Train a team of dedicated workers who stay with you for years, actively helping you bring strategy and tactics in line with each other, than to constantly find and replace people who have no idea why their work matters—and, worse, who couldn't care less.

WHY *DOES* WHAT THEY DO MATTER?

Why am I here? This question is one of the most significant that employees ask themselves when contemplating their jobs. Why do they occupy this particular box in your workplace's organizational chart? What do you, as their leader, expect them to accomplish? What value do they bring to the company?

If they have no real reason for working other than the need to stay busy or provide for their family, then they've lost sight of their workplace mission. While these represent noble objectives, profitable productivity depends on an intimate knowledge of the organization's strategic goals and one's plans for contributing to it.

Most organizations, from Bubba's Bait Shop on Lake Podunk to Ford Motor Company, have an underlying mission driving them toward their goals. A mission consists of a brief, straightforward statement of the organization's primary objectives or bottom-line goals. Bubba's might be, "To sell the best fishing worms in the Greater Tuna area." Ford's could be, "To make the safest cars for the best prices in the U.S.A." Founder Henry Ford's mission was to get inexpensive cars in the hands of the common people, a mission he achieved with flying colors.

What's your organization's mission, and then your department's mission? Do your team members even know, and, if they do, do they care? If the answer to either question is "no," then implement my 4-R Reconnection Strategy to help them realign with these workplace missions.

1. *Reestablish awareness.* Have team members evaluate their current positions by asking, "Which of my activities contribute most of my value to my organization?" If they can't answer that, have them invest personal time in figuring out where they got off course and how they might fix it. Awareness is the first key to progress.

2. *Realign them.* Make sure the mission and their perception of it match up. If employees become misaligned, they may be wasting time on the wrong things. In that case, it doesn't matter how hard they work to get the job done; their productivity will crash. Check back with them regularly to confirm their critical priorities.

3. *Repair their connection.* Once your team members know where they are and where they should be, have them make any necessary course corrections. After that, help them tweak or overhaul their workflow process to get it back on track and in sync with the mission. Specifically, have them make a list of the top five things they think they should be working on, and do the same yourself for each of them. Compare the two lists. Do they match?

4. *Rededicate them to the mission.* Have the team members reaffirm their commitment to your workplace. Help them understand how each contributes to the collective effort to move the organization forward. Whether their contributions prove integral or incre-

mental, make sure they're doing exactly what they should be doing to achieve the long-term strategic objectives of your organization.

Even those who work the hardest will inevitably crash and burn in their productivity if they lose track of the mission. So make sure they look up and regularly check their instruments to see how they're doing. Help them reorient themselves if they've lost their focus on their mission.

BULLDOZE THOSE OBSTACLES!
"[Workers] tend to relate to specific goals and target dates," John Alberto pointed out.

> You put the dates out there, with periodic discussion and course-correction, but basically you give them the vision, the objective—and you step out of their way and let them go for it. If they run into a problem, your job as the leader is to help eliminate that obstacle. You're not giving them the solution; you're helping them come up with the solution on their own. The employee who survives in this environment becomes adept at accelerating, at forward momentum, at drive; they don't really need a whole lot of coaching to be able to move quickly. They don't want to waste a lot of time on stuff that they don't think is important.

Clear the Air
So, what's important to your people? For one thing, they want to know where they stand. They also need to know the basic shape of your strategy and the outcomes you expect them to achieve. Clarifying these outcomes requires you to make some clear, unambiguous decisions about your final destination. Never blindly assume you understand what will happen if you do this as opposed to that. Give

it some deep thought, leveraging not only your experience and intimate knowledge of your marketplace but any other research and information that might affect the outcome. That includes the capabilities of your team members.

Here are four ways to clarify the decision-making process that will result in solid targets for you and your team:

1. *Research the variables.* If you have experience dealing with a particular issue and know for sure the boundary conditions haven't changed, you can confidently proceed with your decision making. However, if you've never dealt with anything like the issue at hand or if conditions are unfamiliar, invest in basic research. If you lack the time to do it yourself, assign it to one of your team members.

2. *Never make unwarranted assumptions.* If someone asks you how long it will take to climb a mountain, don't assume he means Pikes Peak. He might mean Denali. Know for sure what he wants before proceeding. You may find it necessary to solicit help from experts if the course remains unclear.

3. *Set a deadline for action.* Once you've settled the previous factors, set a drop-dead date for making your decision. Announce it to others, so their expectations will force you to work steadily toward it. Otherwise, it might sneak up on you, causing you to make a poor choice.

4. *Start planning.* Develop a better understanding of the issues, determining from there how the project contributes to and aligns with your organizational goals. Conduct outside consultations as necessary. Design and undertake these actions with these goals

in mind: to clarify the outcome of every (reasonable) decision and determine which best benefits your organization.

Once you've covered the major factors, make your decision and make a beeline for the target without letting the devilish details hold you back. As long as you remain flexible, you can handle them as you go. You'll never foresee everything—and you may make the wrong move even after you've done your due diligence. But all business boils down to calculated risk. If pressed, make the best decision you can, even if you're not quite ready. You can always make course corrections later.

To use a delightful old-fashioned phrase, "You pays your money and you takes your chances." But before you pay, make sure you know what you're looking at.

Acknowledge the Churn

Understand and acknowledge that what you're asking your team members to do may require extra work. Make it clear what that work will entail before you invite them to go on that mission with you. After all, you aren't asking them to do a million things; you're focusing on a few key priorities, because that's all you can afford to do. Anything more and you're likely to fail all the way down the line. So meet with your team after selecting the highest-priority issues. Be willing to defend why they're important and enforce your choices.

Here's a good (if minor) example of a leader getting buy-in from the team to accomplish a plan quickly and productively—and it occurred one evening as I was writing this chapter in my home office. Suddenly, the entire neighborhood lost electricity. When the lights went out, my family gathered in the living room in the light of cell phones and my laptop, decided what each person should do to deal with our lightless situation, and did it. Because we've planned for circumstances like this, one person knew to find the flashlights, while another broke out the candles and matches, another took care of our furry "children" to keep them from panicking, and so on.

We calmly handled the situation, and I kept an eye on everyone while they decided how best to achieve their goals and execute their duties. Everyone bought in and got it done. We didn't need a long-term plan. If something had gone awry, the person involved would have let me know, but nothing did. A few minutes later the lights were still out, but the stairs were safe to navigate, the pets were calm, and I was still banging away at the keyboard, writing this book for you, with enough battery power to keep going for hours. Plus, I knew I'd have to eat at least some of that half-gallon of Cookies 'n Cream in the freezer before it melted, so life was good.

All was well because we worked well together, we accepted the extra work required to reach our goals, and we executed our strategy in the most effective manner possible in this "hurry-up epoch": we made the execution itself our strategy. It works for things great and small, from the "family corporation" on up to the multinational.

PAINT A PRETTY PICTURE

In recent years, Cisco Systems has moved to an "open workspace" without walls. If you're a mobile Cisco employee, you come in, you sit down, you work, and then you leave. Two hours later, you may be in another building. You can bring a framed photo of your dog and put it on your desk, but when you leave for the day, you have to take it with you. What was Cisco's mission? To teach employees how to be more flexible and collaborative.

Not everybody was ecstatic about the collaborative workspace. Debbie Gross told me,

> For the longest time, a lot of people were bitching and moaning about it, even me. But people began to see the vision as we continued to talk about it. We painted the picture in their minds: "Can you see the light? Can you feel the airflow? Can you see the energy all around you?" Eventually, people said, "Oh, wow, I get it. Actually, I like it." You want to get them buying into what you're trying to do and getting excited, because once you get them excited, they're going to go along with you and embrace it.
>
> It also allows you to see people, so you can sit in an environment where you can talk to each other. Administrators tend to want to put walls up, and that's not good for the job that they're doing these days either. It's all about reaching out and having lots of communication, and lots of collaboration.

RADIO STATION WII-FM

Motivation will always be an important part of making people care about their work. Whether we admit it to ourselves or not, we all tune into radio station WII-FM: "What's in it for me?" Similarly, your team members are consistently asking themselves, "What will the result of achieving my goals be?" *Every* employee wants that question answered, all the way up and down the line. As Steven Gangwish of CSS Farms told me,

> The final piece of alignment is [that] we have a pretty extensive profit-sharing and bonus program. Our managers know the profitability of their farms, because they're incentivized and compensated based upon that. It's pretty transparent. A sizable amount of their compensation comes from that component. They have long hours and provide excellent service, but when they hit their goals, there is a clear reward tied to

that achievement. If Mother Nature throws a curveball that is outside their control, they're still rewarded.

Our incentive structure is three-fold. The first component is on individual performance. The second component is on the business unit or farm performance. The third component is on the overall company performance. You could have a farm that did all it could do, but then a hailstorm came in and ruined the crop. But the rest of the company did well, despite this one business unit, so even though *their* farm had a bad year, they have other areas to fall back on, or else they would be totally demotivated.

THE FINAL WORD

To create a motivated, empowered team, all members have to care about where they're going and why they should bother. "Because I said so" doesn't cut it anymore, if it ever did. You're not their parent, anyway.

To align team effort with the company's needs and get team members to be more willing to execute your strategy on the fly, show them why what they do matters. Emphasize how their efforts fit within the overall scheme designed to move the organization forward, however incrementally. Spell out why their success and productivity matter to you and the company—and explain the consequences for going off the rails.

You must also demonstrate why what they want matters in the framework of organizational alignment. Acknowledge that the realignment effort may well mean more work for them, at least in the short term. But at the same time, they will have more freedom to achieve than ever before. This is where the whole "Execution IS the Strategy" concept comes into its own. It allows you and your team to grab the ball on the bounce and immediately drive toward the end zone, without getting tangled up in the web of a long-term plan that's outdated the instant it's published.

Here's where your leadership road diverges from the classic dictator of old—that distant leader who handed down directives from on high and expected instant obedience. Instead, modern leaders partner and collaborate with their team members, outlining the vision, facilitating their work, and urging them on. You sculpt the plan and polish it up brightly, laying out the deadlines and the broad outlines before giving team members the ball and letting them run with it.

Your team won't care about anything more than their paychecks unless you inspire them. Get them to care about achieving the organization's goals. If you can do that, come season's end you might end up at your industry's equivalent of the Super Bowl.

Plan for Goal Achievement CHAPTER **8**

People mistrust or distrust the ambiguous—so be crystal clear about what your team members should be accomplishing in their daily activities. When you've communicated your expectations well, you're more likely to get what you want, and everyone is more productive and effective.

Good strategic alignment consists of practices that connect organizational strategy with employee performance as fully and directly as possible. When you properly align your organizational structure, then your employees act as strategic enablers of the company policy, mission, and vision—all working from the same standards toward the same ends. This can only happen when upper management willingly shares its goals with everyone *and* sets up procedures to make sure people stay on track.

While speed is desirable, the whole goal isn't always just move, move, move. You must still take the time to be thoughtful so that you can be more efficient in the long run. Steven Gangwish of CSS Farms told me, "I would say the biggest lesson that I've learned is to make a concerted effort to outline a business plan for each new venture, instead of the Ready, Fire, Aim approach. Oftentimes, just starting on a new project without formally thinking through all of the necessary success factors will slow you down and create rework." He continued:

> By forcing ourselves to be disciplined to write it all down, think through all the risks, and figure out how to mitigate cash outlays, we build optionality into our decision making. I think that has both made us a lot of money and saved us from a lot of losses as we have sought growth opportunities. We make decisions that provide us with the most options at the least cost, and we take the time to research them carefully. Then we can charge forward quickly and confidently.

In the game of business, we keep score with dollars. Profit represents the real-world manifestation of the combination of drive, focus, and efficiency we call productivity. That means ensuring your team members stay busy at what matters and in ways that move everyone toward the prize. Strategic execution ultimately governs productivity.

Let's look at useful strategies for getting into alignment and staying there.

SHARPEN THE STRATEGY SCALPEL
. . . AND START SLICING

We businesspeople have no time for the irrelevant. We certainly can't afford to chase poorly defined goals, so hard-nosed practicality rules. The less important aspects of your work must either take a backseat to the crucial areas or be removed altogether, leaving only the lean, profitable core.

A great example of clarity of focus is McDonald's. Being the number-one fast food chain in every market where it has a presence is its clear goal. Its leaders keep in touch with what's happening around them and where consumers are spending their food dollars, so they can offer the same options less expensively. However, they never wait to see what other restaurants are doing: they create their own destiny. As a result, the McDonald's franchise includes more than 31,000 stores with 1.5 million employees.

What's the most important thing you can do as a leader? Align your company's best interests with team productivity. The best way to do this is with a clear, sharp strategic focus. Apply these six tips to sharpen that focus to laser keenness.

1. *Define your market position.* Assess your current state: fiscal health, market share, infrastructure, and labor costs. Can your resources keep up with current workflow? Do you have enough team members, too few, or too many? Have you invested enough in your infrastructure to stay competitive, or do you overemphasize infrastructure at the expense of production?

2. *Tightly define your mission and vision.* If you can't reduce your goals to a few simple one-line statements, then how can you determine the best route from here to there? A single-minded approach to your work generally works best.

3. *Stay flexible.* Don't be too single-minded; keep enough of an eye on the marketplace to notice when it shifts.

4. *Align your goals.* Get all your ducks in a row, both vertically and horizontally. Everyone needs to know, understand, and align with organizational goals and how to achieve them. They also need to know why and how their efforts matter, so you can engage and empower

them to achieve those goals. Therefore, make a special effort to break down information silos between teams, so no one works at cross-purposes.

5. *Manage performance.* Don't micromanage. Instead, review workplace productivity and overall performance on a regular basis. Take steps to keep the efforts of individual employees pointed in the right direction. Untangle any roadblocks that interfere with the workflow process.

6. *Monitor the metrics.* Watch all important numbers, aiming constantly for improvement. Key metrics will vary according to the organization, but generally, consider the bottom line to be the bottom line. No company can go far if it can't sustain its profitability.

The verb "operate" has numerous definitions, two of which seem especially appropriate here: "to manage or run, as in a business," and "to perform a surgical procedure." To achieve the first, you may have to do the second repeatedly, especially if the body corporate suffers from the cancer of inefficiency. So use the whetstone of these six tips to keep the scalpel of your strategic focus sharp—if only as a form of preventive medicine.

HERE'S THE PLAN . . .

What does a strategic plan look like? It doesn't have to be complex, as long as you make all the basics clear: mission, vision, goals, and the pathways you plan to use to get there. It can be as simple as a single-page document. For example, at the National Speakers Association (NSA), where I was privileged to serve as president from 2011 to 2012, our strategic plan is simple—a single matrix that outlines the important goals and how we plan to accomplish them during the course of the year. Remember, rigid, long-term, complex plans just don't work in today's business environment.

According to Stacy Tetschner, CEO of the NSA,

> Our leadership has changed the way we develop and execute our core strategies and strategic plan. Our strategic plan became the three-year projection for what we wanted to see accomplished in the association at the highest level. We kept it simple enough to fit on one page. We knew what was to be accomplished by when. Then we could easily break it down to operational plans to be executed by the management team. We then developed one-year operational plans that were again highly measurable and made marked progress toward each individual strategy we had developed in the larger three-year plan.
>
> Our board of directors then made the decision to embrace a new oversight philosophy. Instead of being involved in guiding the tactical execution, they served as advisors for clarity and occasionally ideas, and turned over the implementation and execution of these plans to the staff. Our working title for this transition was "Volunteer Advised and Staff Managed." Overall, this helped the organization move from different strategies that were developed with only a one-year focus to a plan that carried on no matter which volunteers happened to be in leadership roles that year.

In another example, Debbie Gross of Cisco said, "We have tools within our system where everybody can input their goals and objectives; I have five, for example." She continued,

> Everything starts with our overall mission: to be the top communications/IT company. Then it rolls to a three-to-five-year goal such as, "The network is the platform. Integrate technology and business architecture." Next, I determine how my role aligns as an administrative professional.

It means I will have to become more customer-centric, customer-focused. No, I'm not going to build the technology that does that. But when I'm interfacing with a customer, I'm going to give my best support. Because I'm seen as a leader for the administrative teams, they now have the option of looking at my goals and objectives. For example, "Continued educational development" is one of mine, so I can continue my learning in the technology field. They can tie their goals into mine and tweak them to apply in their worlds.

START MOVING AND HOLD ON TIGHT

As a leader, you tell your team where you're going and what you want to do. The responsibility then lies with each team member to say, "Given my role, here's what I know, and here's what I recommend."

Occasionally, you'll sit down with each team member individually and review his or her goals and objectives, asking for clarifications. If someone isn't going in the right direction or has veered off course, it's up to you to get that person back on track. As with geese flying in formation, you can't have one goose going its own way, because that reduces the strength of the overall formation.

By now, it's probably clear that annual performance reviews aren't sufficient. Yet too much control can become micromanagement—the exact opposite of high productivity. So how do you find a happy medium? How do you connect each employee's execution of the work to the organization's overall vision? How do you create a comfortable level of strategic alignment resulting in profit, growth, and all-around success?

In the next few sections, we'll look at ideas that help achieve all this.

Nothing's set in stone. Once you establish a plan, you'll have to make adjustments to mirror the changes in strategy

NSA Three Year Strategic Plan (2014–2016)

Learn

NSA's Strategies: ↓

Strategic Objectives: ⟶

Education

Create and deliver content-rich, industry-leading programming, events, products and services at all levels to meet revenue, membership and participation targets.

Year 1: 2014 **Learn • Grow • Share** (Ink) • Increase the speed of implementation on strategies • Clarify our Vision - who we are • Clarify/Refine membership criteria & focus of benefits, programs and services • Clarify & communicate NSA's value proposition • Raise the bar on our programming & services • Implement the volunteer advised/staff managed philosophy across all programs • Solidify NSA's finanical operating position	✓ Conduct Member Needs Assessment. ✓ Redesign and elevate educational offerings and support structure. ✓ Hire and develop staff with expertise and depth of knowledge to achieve stated goals. ✓ Develop technology to support education efforts. ✓ Enhance chapter educational offerings. ✓ Design financially self supportive programs and events.
Year 2: 2015 **Learn • Grow • Share** (Pencil) • Implement first full year of revised strategies and track impact • Utilize research from member needs assessment to develop relevant and valuable programming • Assess staffing needs and current positioning • Develop plans for investing undesignated funds in future strategic/value focused programs and benefits	✓ Develop tools to track impact of revised educational strategies and offerings. ✓ Transition all educational offerings to volunteer advised/staff managed model. ✓ Fully absorb all costs of staffing (Learning Director) into operating budget. ✓ Implement year 2 technology plan for education from three year plan.
Year 3: 2016 **Learn • Grow • Share** (Whiteboard) • Assess and refine plan, services, programs to maximize Member ROI • Assess staffing levels and needs for future development • Plan for budgets based on 2 year history with new strategic planning structure • Continually monitor and model technology trends to position NSA as a leader for presentation and entrepreneurial technologies	✓ Implement final aspects of digital delivery technologies (i.e. apps, YouTube channels, etc.). ✓ Utlilize processes to monitor and implement trends in education and delivery to position NSA as the leader of the profession. ✓ Use digital delivery models to begin phase out of CD and DVD offerings. ✓ Implement year 3 technology plan for education from three year plan.

VISION: Every expert who presents content to an audience through the spoken word for a fee belongs to NSA.

MISSION: NSA is the leading source for education, community, and entrepreneurial business knowledge needed to be successful in the speaking profession.

Grow	Share
Entrepreneurship Model and share business practices and technologies that help members create sustainable businesses and develop their expertise.	**Community** Create a community that helps the Association meet its membership and participation targets.

✓ Conduct Member Needs Assessment. ✓ Revise certification (CSP) program. ✓ Create technology to support entrepreneurship efforts. ✓ Develop stronger chapter business model. ✓ Rebrand NSA convention as a business event. ✓ Identify and pursue members that best support NSA business model.	✓ Conduct Member Needs Assessment. ✓ Transition to segmented offerings through Professional Delivery Groups (PDG). ✓ Develop technology to support community building efforts. ✓ Aggressively recruit new, targeted members. ✓ Invest in development of benefit programs identified in member needs assessment.
✓ Evaluate and implement entrepreneurship needs from year 1 assessment. ✓ Implement revised CSP certification program. ✓ Position NSA as a stronger resource for best practices in association management for chapters. ✓ Implement convention branding efforts.	✓ Refine and enhance targeted member recruitment. ✓ Develop PDG governance structure to better align volunteer resources with delivery of PDG program benefits. ✓ Implement Year 2 community plans from 3-year technology plan.
✓ Develop further partnerships with associations and businesses that provide relevant entrepreneurial business practice solutions for speakers. ✓ Conduct business needs assessment for NSA chapters to better align NSA chapter education programs with needs of the volunteer leaders.	✓ Implement Year 3 community plans from 3-year technology plan. ✓ Refine and enhance continued focus on member recruitment.

NSA Year 1
Operational Plan (2013–2014)

Learn

Operational Strategies:

Strategic Objectives: ⟶

Education
Create and deliver content-rich, industry-leading programming, events, products and services at all levels to meet revenue, membership and participation targets.

Member Services
Research and develop a comprehensive offering of relevant member benefits and services that provide value to our members and fulfill our Mission.

1. Conduct in-depth member needs market assessment. *(In process – deliver 7/25/13)*
2. Hire Director of Learning Experiences. *(Complete by 7/15/13)*
3. Convene the Education Redevelopment Team at 2014 Convention. *(June 2014)*
4. Elevate main stage, breakout and *Speaker*/VOE talent. *(On-going)*
5. Develop an NSA branded YouTube Channel to share education tips, practices and programs. *(Spring 2014 – no progress yet.)*

Chapter Relations
Enhance the relationship between NSA and its chapters to better reflect the brand image of the organization through chapters as local gatherings of NSA members and provide a consistent high-value experience for all members and guests.

1. Share best practices for education program speakers, delivery and design for use among NSA chapters. *(Planning for revised Chapter One site in process – deliver February 2014.)*
2. Determine next steps in merger of National and Chapter Academy programs. *(Template has been shared / best practices being collected – deliver November 2013.)*

Marketing
Create and communicate an aggressive, clear value proposition that helps the Association meet its revenue, membership and participation targets.

1. Fund and implement education marketing plan. *(In process for 2014 meetings and events.)*

VISION: Every expert who presents content to an audience through the spoken word for a fee belongs to NSA.

MISSION: NSA is the leading source for education, community, and entrepreneurial business knowledge needed to be successful in the speaking profession.

Grow	Share
Entrepreneurship	**Community**
Model and share business practices, technologies, and trends that help members create sustainable businesses and develop their expertise.	Create a community that helps the Association meet its membership and participation targets.

1. Conduct in-depth member needs market assessment. *(In process – complete 7/25/13)* 2. Implement revised CSP criteria to better reflect current speaking business practice. *(Complete)* 3. Create and develop an NSA branded YouTube Channel to share education tips, practices and programs to include entrepreneurial business knowledge focus. *(Spring 2014 – no progress yet)*	1. Conduct in-depth member needs market assessment. *(In process – complete 7/25/13)* 2. Transition PEG program to Professional Delivery Group program (PDG). *(In process – complete 7/14/13)* 3. Implement segmentation program by PDG program. *(July 2014)* 4. Create and develop an NSA branded YouTube Channel to share programs that will enhance the NSA community experience. *(Spring 2014)*
1. Support Chapter Leadership Teams throughout the year by sharing Association management insights and best practices. *(Deliver June 2014.)*	1. Create and facilitate Chapter Leader social media groups to encourage sharing of ideas and best practices. *(Deliver February 2014.)*
1. Develop a national brand for NSA's annual convention that attracts speakers seeking to grow their existing business. *(Merged with a new brand strategy for NSA November 2013. In process – complete November 2013.)*	1. Fund and implement member recruitment and retention marketing plan that includes qualifying prospects for appropriate segments of engagement with the Association *(In process – ongoing with no specific completion date.)* 2. Finalize tiers of strategy with focus on business "maturity" (i.e. Emerging, Experienced and Enterprise level speakers). *(Currently being reconsidered for feasibility in current fiscal year.)*

Learn

Education

Create and deliver content-rich, industry-leading programming, events, products and services at all levels to meet revenue, membership and participation targets.

Operational Strategies: ↓

Strategic Objectives: ⟶

Technology

Be supported by a robust technological backbone that delivers valuable educational and member experiences while enhancing performance, distribution and influence.

1. Fund and implement year one educational elements of 3-year technology plan. *(Complete)*
   a. *Speaker* magazine app
   b. VOE app *(Being delivered July 2013.)*

Financial

Be fiscally positioned to enable the operating budget to fund annual operations that support the Association's growth as well as the strategic plan.

1. Create at least break-even budgets for each strategic event, with corresponding financial projections and profit & loss statements generated at the end of the event. *(Complete)*

Grow	Share
Entrepreneurship	**Community**
Model and share business practices, technologies, and trends that help members create sustainable businesses and develop their expertise.	Create a community that helps the Association meet its membership and participation targets.

Grow	Share
1. Fund and implement year one entrepreneurial business knowledge aspects of 3-year tech plan. a. ID and sharing of speaker business technology trends *(Complete July 2014)*	1. Fund and implement year one community building aspects of 3-year technology plan. *(Large increase in social media participation. Speaker magazine blog – complete June 2013. Website redesign in process – complete by February 2014.)* 2. Develop online assessment for segmentation and targeted value offerings. *(Currently being reconsidered for feasibility in current fiscal year.)*

Grow	Share
1. Assess who are most profitable members to the Association: Emerging, Expanding or Enterprise members; and, determine ROI and future actions, products and services for each group. *(Currently being reconsidered for feasibility in current fiscal year.*	1. Develop plan to invest undesignated assets into member services programs based on needs assessment. *(Complete – February 2013)*

necessitated by real-world (r)evolutions in your industry. You may have to respond almost instantly to take advantage of a short-term opportunity. Even if you don't respond, well, things will still change incrementally on an almost-daily basis. How you adjust will determine how well you survive.

Consider Microsoft, whose game programmers receive real-time feedback from online consumers like my teenage sons. Players are executing in the moment, and their feedback soon bubbles up to the programming leaders, constantly shaping new priorities and the way they spend their time. Often, this stimulates brand-new concepts that improve gameplay and customer satisfaction.

How can you manage a similar process as a leader in your company? How do you support the team members who actually keep their ears to the ground and know what's going on?

This can be complicated, if only because the process requires a constant awareness of what's happening in your field. You can't afford to get so involved in the day-to-day execution that you lose track of what your audience wants.

For example, if you're a game designer and look up one day only to realize that gaming has moved on to an entirely different meme, then your fabulous new game may be dead out of the box. Game developer John Romero learned this to his chagrin with *Daikatana II*. His company hyped the game to epic (and somewhat offensive) proportions before its many delays, cost overruns, and poor project management left it so far behind the times that it lost its window of opportunity—and flopped miserably when finally released.

Milestones represent an important part of any plan, but you must pay close attention to determine if where you're headed still matters. Check in with your people regularly.

Are they still aligned with the organization? If not, who seems to be headed in the wrong direction—the team, or the organization as a whole? Are you unaware of a new initiative that has put the company on a new heading? You'd better find out so you can take the helm if necessary.

I recommend you pull out your spyglass and check the seas ahead to make sure you're not about to enter a storm—or, worse, run aground on the shoals. I can't overstate the value of investing the time necessary to regularly and religiously check your team's course. Make even the tiniest course corrections if you think they're needed.

THE CRUCIAL PARADOX:
TENACITY AND LETTING GO

Leaders at all levels must consistently attempt to keep the plan current. Things will change, sometimes drastically enough to knock the plan so askew that it no longer fits the situation. Thus, every organization needs to build a framework that embraces and integrates changes into its plan.

Cisco leadership uses Operating Committees to bring together executives to examine their strategic priorities. If they aren't getting where they need to be, they ask why. In some cases, they have to cut their losses and let go of some people or pieces of the business. As Debbie Gross told me,

> You must be able to let go, to say, "This is holding us back. This is not working." Being in love with something can be your biggest issue; it slows you down and has big financial consequences if you can't move quickly enough.
>
> If you carry baggage too long, it's going to weigh you down. If you start seeing red in the bottom line, you have to cut it out—it's not going to bring you any more success. Once you realize that, you have to let it go.

Debbie brings up a good point. As much as it goes against the grain for most businesspeople, sometimes the most productive action you can take is to give up. As a leader, canceling failing projects may be one of your most important secondary responsibilities.

But how can you tell when you should let go of a project that's weighing you down? After all, a project's failure may still produce an unexpected success. Alexander Fleming discovered penicillin after a failed experiment with *Staphylococcus* bacteria (mostly because he failed to clean his Petri dishes before going on vacation, oddly enough). And 3M initially rejected the adhesive later used on Post-it® Notes because it wasn't sticky enough.

You need a benchmark to measure against. So in a standard business context, let's define a failing project as something that:

- Doesn't work as intended.

- Goes too far over budget.

- Won't (or can't) be delivered on time.

Watch for these seven common indicators:

1. *Poorly defined requirements.* If you can't get the project sponsors to take enough interest to clarify their requirements, then you're in trouble from the start. A one-line requirements document that says something like, "We want an easy-to-use scoreboard system" won't cut it. Prod the clients to tell you precisely what they need, and keep asking until they do. If they never do, you might as well shut it down, because you can't guarantee you'll hit the mark.

2. *Unrealistic scheduling or budgeting.* Projects need realistic, well-defined schedules and budgets that in-

clude reasonable milestones for each. I know a professional editor who occasionally receives bid requests
with requirements such as, "I need my four-hundred-
page novel edited within two weeks for $500." A de-
cent edit for a four-hundred-page novel takes at least
three times that long and four times the proffered rate.
Someone somewhere may take the project, but the
writer won't get quality work in return. Conversely,
schedules that seem ridiculously long and lack deadlines risk letting the project fall by the wayside in favor
of more urgent projects, while a budget that burns
through money may doom a project to failure as well.

3. *High cash-burn rate.* Speaking of burning through
   money, how's your cost performance index (CPI), otherwise known as your earned value divided by actual
   cost? If it falls below 1 for too long, your budget is out
   of control (assuming there's no change in schedule or
   scope). For example, suppose you spend $100,000 on
   a direct mail campaign that nets only $50,000 over
   the course of a year. That's a cash-burn rate you can't
   afford to maintain.

4. *Scope creep.* When you receive a project, it should
   state clearly what you need to deliver and when. If
   the client keeps saying, "Hey, while you're in there,
   can you add this too?" then you may suffer from scope
   creep. The project grows and grows, often without a
   corresponding budget increase or schedule adjustment.

5. *Bad attitude.* Does your team think the project is a
   waste of time? Do you have trouble pinning down the
   client or your own manager because neither seems to
   care? Do the intended users seem uncommitted to the
   project or even actively hostile? Do *you* feel curiously
   ambivalent? If so, red alert!

6. *High churn rate.* People who leave a project take their skills and knowledge with them. You then have to train someone new or redistribute the load to others. Either way, the project loses momentum and speed; up goes the cost, down goes the value. In time, the CPI may be so low that you have no other choice but to quit.

7. *Failures.* You may find that your creation doesn't work right or well enough for some reason. Suppose the accounting department has tasked you to build a new database. Beta and acceptance testing might reveal problems you can't reliably or economically repair. Or you may discover halfway into the project that XYZ Corporation's brand-new database works better for a lower cost. Or technology may simply advance so fast that the project becomes outdated before its release. Technology companies like Research in Motion, Apple, and Android constantly duke it out in the courts over "patent infringements" that may have occurred simply because of parallel and uncorrelated product development.

Finally, don't fall prey to the "sunk cost" fallacy. Just because you've sunk a lot of time, effort, and cash into a project, that doesn't mean you can't unplug and walk away whenever you need to. In some cases you must, if only to avoid throwing good money after bad. So end it gracefully. Coordinate with the client or sponsors to determine the proper procedure for project cancellation. Then let the project team and other stakeholders know. Return or release any remaining budget, wrap up basic tasks, and document the closure. Someday, someone may learn or even rescue something of value from your failure.

LASER SURGERY FOR YOUR COMPANY

Communication

By now, you may have noticed a common thread running through this book—the value of frank, open communication in everything you do. Too many business relationships have floundered owing to a lack of clear, bidirectional communication. Like many other things in the professional world, successful business alignment starts with good communication.

Suppose your boss gestures vaguely at the horizon and says, "Our goal is to climb that mountain over there." Which mountain does he mean? Does he have a method and schedule in mind? If he doesn't clarify, you'd better ask. It won't help the bottom line if you end up climbing the wrong mountain.

As a leader, you have a duty to share your organization's strategic goals with your team members as plainly as possible. Bring them up to date on everything relevant—from long-term targets down to the daily adjustments that keep you on course. While you needn't reveal every little detail, the broad outlines should be transparent to all. That way, people can see the general strategy, where they fit into its framework, and how their efforts help move everyone closer to the final destination.

Many of us have had jobs in which we had no idea where we were going or whether what we did even mattered. A business can survive this; it may even make money at it. But you can rest assured that productivity will limp along, uninspired at best. If you keep your team members in the dark, you run the risk of creating unhappy drones—the ones who either waste their time or sit muttering in their cubicles guarding their staplers. Remember poor Milton in the movie *Office Space*, who ended up burning the place down?

So communicate with your team members clearly and completely, lest you figuratively "burn down" your own business. Give them the information and other tools they need to get the job done. Let them ask any and all questions they deem necessary, and answer them patiently. Then make sure you ask a few of your own to test *their* understanding of your goals. Along the way, take advantage of all available methods of communication, from team meetings to instant messaging.

On a broader scale, communicating your basic strategy can be as easy as publishing a brief mission/vision/core values statement on the company intranet, or circulating a memo that everyone on the team must sign off on. Most businesses give new employees a handbook outlining company policy in exhaustive detail. Invest even more time orienting your team members to the company's strategic goals, your related goals, and their important role in achieving them.

Clear communication of strategic goals represents just one leg of a successful alignment effort. A solid structure requires at least two others: education and oversight. All three support and reinforce the others. Weakness or failure in any destabilizes the entire effort.

Education

A smart organization provides its employees with basic strategic guidelines right along with procedural and occupational training. This falls under the heading of giving your people the tools they need to do their jobs correctly.

Education about strategic goals doesn't have to take long. Simply show your workers where they fit into the grand scheme of things and emphasize why their work matters. This demonstrates their value to the company, which will motivate them, and, with any luck, increase their level of engagement. Make it clear to everyone—from the youngest intern to senior managers—that the work each is responsible for has importance if it moves the organization toward its strategic goals.

Oversight

In the 1990s, we used to talk about SMART objectives— how they had to be Specific, Measurable, Attainable, Relevant, and Timely. Now we've gotten SMARTER, having added Evaluate and Reevaluate to the acronym.

This implies that individual workers must consistently justify their ROIs by demonstrating their contributions toward achieving group goals. Therefore, once you've defined the company direction and provided the tools employees need to get there, check in with them regularly (as noted earlier). You want to make sure they're executing your business strategy effectively.

For example, my assistant Becca sits at her desk and works for hours every day. I don't look over her shoulder constantly (actually, I usually don't talk with her at all, because I'm generally traveling to see a client or speaking at a conference). So, as her manager, how do I know I'm getting the best possible ROI out of her efforts? How do I know if what she's working on today will achieve the company's objectives in three months? Training and communicating my goals aren't enough; I also need to make sure Becca's execution stays on target. We must check in on key milestones daily, weekly, and monthly.

Then, too, how do I make sure she has the space and time she needs to work on her tasks? I have to provide both. Similarly, if you want people to be strategic enablers of business, you have to give them time to be strategic (versus running around putting out brush fires and never having time to do anything important).

One more thing about oversight: organizations require transparency from the top down, but transparency in the other direction can be valuable, too.

Employees like to know how their performance affects the organization as a whole. If Bob Smith helped the company get a $5 million contract last month, he'd certainly want to see how it translates up the ladder. Many organizations routinely conceal such information, but doing so can negatively affect employee engagement. Poor engagement may hurt strategic alignment. So if, for example, Bob suspects someone else got credit for his work or the company went nowhere despite his efforts, his attitude and productivity might suffer.

How can you ensure mutual trust and flow in both directions? Your organization could provide a measurement system that lets both you and your employees track performance. If you don't have it, create your own.

For example, using regular written weekly activity reports (WARs) might work. You could conduct informal weekly and formal quarterly reviews instead of yearly reviews. Having shared online workspaces has become common: you could use Microsoft Outlook Task Assignments, SharePoint, or Google Docs to implement a shared tracking system. These allow easy tracking of both an individual's day-to-day productivity as well as points of progress toward specific objectives.

COMMUNICATION + EDUCATION + OVERSIGHT = COHERENCE

Did you know the word "laser" was originally an acronym for Light Amplification by Stimulated Emission of Radiation? Normal light bounces all over the place, but a laser makes light waves line up in one direction only. Scientists call this "coherence." The coherent light beam emerges from the laser so tightly focused that, if it's powerful enough, it can punch through steel.

Let's apply that to the workplace. When combined with the right strategic training and oversight, transparent communication of organizational goals encourages workplace coherence. It acts as a force multiplier that yields a synergistic whole greater than the sum of its parts. Employees slot easily into teams that link readily to advance group goals with a minimum of wasted energy. As a result, they produce brilliant, focused light rather than useless heat and noise.

Another beneficial result is agility in decision making. When everyone knows exactly where to go and how to get there, making decisions becomes simple and fast. Taken together, all this results in a flexible production machine in which individual "parts" move with one unified purpose— like a school of fish or flock of birds.

Still, individuality remains important, because the machine only works when employees enjoy enough empowerment to willingly engage in teamwork and take initiative. When they do, it benefits everyone.

In contrast, slow decision making occurs when people are confused about where to go and how best to get there. Ever been in a meeting where people hash over an issue repeatedly, but the attendees still leave without agreements in place? Frustrations prevail; productivity dives.

BOTTOMS UP! (GOALS, THAT IS)

In the past, the leaders at the top handed down goals from on high. The officers informed the directors, who informed the managers, who informed the supervisors, who informed the employees. Today, goals often bubble up from below. Leaders can't easily create "strategic goals"; only those who execute them can own those goals. Hence, execution—or at least the team that executes—*is* the strategy.

These days, leaders create the strategic priorities that shape the goals and draft blueprints based on the team's recommendations. Then their team members do the building.

This puts the onus on the leader to refrain from concluding that a goal has been created until the execution team adopts that goal. Thus, the leader's job is to ask his or her team, "What tactics can you adopt that will get us there?" From there, the idea is to keep the conversation going as a positive feedback loop. That way, the team can shift goals and tactics as circumstances require.

A good case study of a failure of this process is Nokia, which once dominated the cell phone market. This company had the best software and hardware execution team in the business. It could have beaten Apple's iPhone to the market by about two years—if its leaders had set that as a goal. However, senior management decided the strategic goal of the company was profitability and killed the idea of pursuing smartphones—an idea bubbling up from below—because "dumb phones" were so much more profitable at the time.

Looking through the lens of 20/20 hindsight, that proved to be a remarkably dumb move. Among other things, the thousands of smart, gifted employees who could have delivered on the goal of dominating the smartphone market mostly left the company—and Nokia ran into a brick wall when the iPhone came out. The company never recovered. If its strategic priority had been, "How can we be the sales and innovation leader in cell phones?" its teams could have delivered the goals to achieve that priority. The innovators in research and development were infinitely smarter than those in the upper echelons about what the company's goals should have been.

What's the lesson here? Don't just assume the executive

leaders know best. As the Nokia fiasco proved, they sometimes don't. Get out there and find out what you should be
doing differently, not only in terms of mechanical invention but also in terms of process and workflow.

Debbie Gross told me her boss, John Chambers, Cisco's CEO, constantly works on "getting to the core," as she
called it. "He has learned that the hierarchical structure is
not always the right way to get the information he needs,
so he spends a lot of time deep within the organization.
He talks directly to the development engineers. He runs
forums to hear their issues, hear their excitement, and hear
their ideas. Then he takes that information and runs it back
up to the leaders."

In the 2012 holiday season, Chambers walked the halls
with candy and gathered people around, listening to them
and their ideas. Debbie said,

> He came back with copious notes and said, "We shouldn't
> have done that. That was not a good decision. Everyone I
> talked with complained about it." He's very different from
> some CEOs in that respect. He gets his information from the
> top down and from the bottom up, and then everything comes
> together based on mutual decision.
>
> Ultimately, it's a team decision. It's one of the ways that
> he has learned to really keep this company moving in the right
> direction.

To maximize the value of your team members—including their reservoirs of knowledge, experience, and innovation—get out of your ivory tower and walk the halls. Visit
the places your frontline employees dwell. When you hang
out where they get the real work done, that's where you
get the best temperature readings. That's also where you
feel the pulse, discover the pain points, and find out what's
really going on.

Good leaders take their own experience, knowledge, and perspective, and fuse it with all they've heard in the trenches to make decisions that work best for the company.

THE FINAL WORD

I cannot overstate the importance of aligning your strategic focus with carefully designed organizational goals. Properly implemented, this practice removes bottlenecks, breaks down information silos, cuts redundancy, limits confusion, and maximizes productivity. Working well requires a high level of coherence, made up of the proper measures of communication, education, and oversight.

Needless to say, one size does not fit all. How much of each ingredient you should add to your "alignment recipe" depends on the nature and size of your organization. Determining the right amounts requires careful testing, undertaken with a clear-eyed willingness to learn.

Moreover, goal-setting should no longer be limited to the company executives; it's clear that leaders don't always know best. Part of the "Execution IS the Strategy" philosophy arises from letting frontline employees take the ball and carry it forward when the solution is obvious to them. This is true especially when the rate of change doesn't allow time for a classic trickledown of goals from the top.

What really matters, in the end, is getting there—the topic of chapter 9.

Measure Your Progress

S trategic planning and goal setting must be linked, with everyone on the team having goals that support the plan *and* each other.

Not only do all involved have to do the day-to-day tactical tasks that drive the operation, but they also have to work on the higher-level strategic goals as well—the parts that will eventually become their daily work. Along the way, they must constantly assess whether the tasks they complete in the short term will get them where they need to go in the long term.

As Janie Wade from Baylor Health Care explained,

> Our annual goal-setting process starts from the executive team and cascades down to frontline staff. Everyone's goals fit into Service, People, Finance, or Quality. Before goals are finalized, managers review them among teams to ensure cooperation. If John has a goal to decrease supply expense per case and Mary has to do something for him to accomplish it, then Mary's goals have to include this work. Their managers make sure they're both being measured on this goal.

Our performance management software has an employee's annual goals loaded into it along with ninety-day plans, so the employee can load tactics to achieving those goals. We report metrics (as compared to the goal) as frequently as we can. Some metrics can only be tracked on a monthly basis, but others can be monitored daily. Frequency depends on how automated the tracking is.

Let's take a closer look at the concept of metrics, and how it might apply to your organization.

A LITTLE OF THIS, A LITTLE OF THAT

How do we measure a company's success? By the number of fulfilled yet ambitious colleagues? Impressive profits? Positive reception of new initiatives? Satisfied shareholders (if there is such a thing)?

Definitions may shift based on the size of the business, the time of year, and even on the type of leaders you envision yourself and your co-executives to be. Also, definitions of success differ as the focus changes owing to circumstances and how both the marketplace and technology evolve.

As an analogy, consider this: Even after a century of constant refinement, flying an airplane remains a hazardous occupation. Pilots must pay constant attention to altitude, direction, speed, and potential obstacles. This holds true whether they can see for a hundred miles or no farther than the cockpit's windshield. So how do they maintain contact with reality when they can see nothing but clouds? By flying with instruments—a requirement every pilot must master. Pilots monitor the compass, altimeter, horizon indicator, speedometer, and a dozen other instruments, while using radio and radar to check their position.

As a business leader, you have a lot in common with pilots. You're flying the team plane on a tactical mission toward your organizational goals; you can't always see clearly where you're going; and it's potentially hazardous if you fail. So you also have to pay constant attention to your course, making every effort to pierce the fog between you and your goals. As my father taught me when I learned to drive, "Always check your six."

In his Air Force parlance (assuming a horizontal clock with twelve o'clock immediately ahead), "six" represents the area directly behind you. My father meant for me to be aware of everything going on around me, not only what was immediately in front of me.

You have to check your "six" at work, too, keeping an eye on the environment and what's looming on the horizon. Although the business equivalents of piloting instruments rarely operate in real-time, keeping an eye on what I call the "Check Six Measures" can help you maintain appropriate levels of accountability and clarity as you move your team toward its destination.

What are the six measures?

1. *Cash flow.* These two words can mean the life or death of an organization. Many entrepreneurs view business as a game, with money as the means of keeping score—a simplistic viewpoint, but a sensible one. Consider your company's cash flow as your altimeter. How high are you flying? Does income exceed expenses by an ample margin? If not, is that your engine you hear sputtering?

2. *Budget and schedule.* How efficiently do your employees do their jobs? Is group workflow so smooth and orderly that everyone turns in their projects on schedule or sooner? Do you complete them on or under budget?

3. *Quality of work.* Even if your other readings look great, you can still run into a mountain if you drift off

course. Who cares if you consistently come in under schedule and budget if the quality of your output stinks?

4. *Hours worked per process.* In many businesses, labor is the highest input cost. Assuming your organization pays its workers a fixed salary rather than by the hour, you can always meet budget and schedule by having people work longer hours. But overworking people presents its own butcher's bill. Would you trust your life to a pilot expected to fly twelve hours straight for ten days in a row?

5. *Customer satisfaction.* This "instrument" works equally well whether your customer base consists of millions of people or a handful of executives. Your superiors will surely let you know if you fail to meet their expectations; the general public may not be so responsive. However, you can encourage a reading of this metric by circulating surveys among your customers. Do they want to continue flying with you?

6. *Return on investment.* ROI acts as the speedometer of your workplace cockpit, tying the rest of your metrics together. How healthy is your ROI? How will achieving the metrics laid out in the bonus plan impact the bottom line? Are you paying out more than you'll save? Be sure to keep everything well maintained; don't cut corners just to save a buck. And never grab for the brass ring at the expense of the gold one that waits a bit farther along the path.

The Check Six Measures aren't the only ways to determine whether you and your employees have succeeded in executing your organizational strategy. Still, they offer a good place to start. Once you've got them in place and have a good idea of your overall situation, you can add and subtract specific metrics as conditions require. But you do need to guard against excessive controls, lest they stymie innovation in the process.

PLAY IT BY EAR

Everyone has a different idea about how to best execute a task, which means that any given team member would probably run a play differently than you would. But that's okay, as long as the team reaches the end zone. How the players move the ball down the field isn't nearly as important as scoring. So you basically need to tell them, "Here's where we're going. I trust you; you're competent. How will you get us there?"

Not all the decisions your team members make will be the right ones, and you'll probably need to course-correct along the way. As leader, one of your jobs is to keep everyone moving in the right direction while letting them do it their way. You can't continue doing pieces for them, or they'll never learn to run the ball. But they'll "score" when you say, "I like your idea on how to go there. That's where I want to go, so lead the way."

"I'm not going to get too granular while I track my team's progress," said Mike Howard from Microsoft in our interview.

> That's the bane of management in corporate America. Leaders micromanage their folks' execution plans. You have to monitor wisely, yes, but you have to give them the latitude to do their work. Otherwise, they won't feel empowered to do it. They'll just think, "The boss is going to double-check everything I do anyway. I have no authority here—I'm just a cog in the wheel."
>
> To me, leadership is the symbiotic relation between environment and alignment. If you have the right environment,

not only will the alignment work, but it will also free up people to think outside the box. If everyone is thinking, *I have to execute on what Mike told me to do and how to do it*, as opposed to, *Okay, I know I can do it, but let me try another idea I just thought about* . . . That's how you get ideas flowing, and maybe you'll get some innovations out of that.

It's a fine balance, but you have to find that sweet spot to allow execution with the ability to innovate. Let them figure out the best way to achieve your vision, and inform you. You'll get more creativity by staying out of their way.

WHAT DO YOU MEAN, STRATEGY AND TACTICS AREN'T THE SAME?

In modern business, many of us are still executing on old strategies that tie down those actually doing the work with specific tactics for doing so. That may work at McDonald's, where the goal is speed and consistency and where leadership has everything down to a science. But most businesses don't work that way, and in fact they can't in the modern marketplace.

We mere humans can only try to anticipate and keep up. This requires a certain flexibility of approach in which tactics take a back seat to the execution of the strategy—no matter what it takes to execute it. Just because you've traditionally done something a certain way doesn't mean it's still the best way (if it ever was). So constantly review your strategy, challenge the staff to innovate, and be open to change when they do.

Wise leaders possess a profound understanding of the difference between strategy and tactics, knowing exactly what each involves. Again, strategy is long-term thinking—the framework organizing what you do over months or years to achieve your goals. Tactics represent the individual steps toward those goals—the things you do today to prepare for tomorrow.

Suppose your *objective* is to visit every country in the European Union over the course of a summer. You'll need a *strategy*; let's say beginning in Spain and moving east to Cyprus before curving up and around to the U.K. and Ireland. Your *tactics* might include buying a Eurail pass, pinpointing hostel locations, taking cabs when necessary, deciding where you'll stop to eat and sleep, and so on.

No doubt you can make the distinction between strategy and tactics in business, but can your team members? Some probably can, but have no choice but to focus on the operational activities required to keep the money flowing. So how do you also get them to invest time on long-term strategies—the important-but-not-urgent activities that make the difference between spinning their wheels and actually getting somewhere?

To make sure your team keeps moving forward with an appropriate mix of strategy and tactics, implement these four practices in your group.

1. *Communicate.* Now, there's a familiar word, reemphasized here because it's crucial. Make everyone aware of the big goal, and precisely what you need them to do to move the team toward that goal. Publish group objectives in memos or on the company intranet, then publicly keep track of your group's progress. This can be both inspirational and motivational.

2. *Engage.* Help your employees care about their work, so you'll have an easier time keeping them on track. Give them incentives: if they know rewards are waiting down the line, most will make extra efforts to ensure the organization's strategic goals come to pass.

3. *Empower.* Give your team members the power to make life easier not only for themselves but for the entire team. Encourage them to take the initiative to

improve group efficiency in ways that pave the road to long-term success.

4. *Provide.* If you need to pound in a nail and all you have is a wrench, sure, you can do it—but not efficiently. Get a hammer to do the job right. Similarly, make sure your people have the proper tools to accomplish their tasks, so they can build a framework for future success. If someone needs a new computer, supply it. If someone needs training, invest in the training. Using the right tools and resources improves their Engagement and Empowerment quotients.

Maintain a firm grasp on the difference between strategy and tactics, while educating your employees on the distinction as well. When they care enough, they'll keep an eye on the profit horizon, not just on the task in front of them.

WALK THE TIGHTROPE . . . WHILE JUGGLING

Good leadership requires a continual balancing act. On the one hand, you've got to keep the team fueled up and running smoothly on a day-to-day basis; on the other, you have to look into your crystal ball and plan for the future. For those occupying the C-suite, the stakes become especially high.

Which function should demand the majority of your time: short-term tactics or long-term strategy, assuming you've wisely delegated or jettisoned everything else? This question goes straight to the heart of the leader's chief reason for existing.

Let's look at four points to help you make your decision.

1. *Good news/bad news.* The bad news first: there's no clear-cut answer here. It depends on the job. The good

news: as crazy-fast as the business world has become,
tactics and strategy have begun to merge into a continuum, rather than presenting as distinct entities.
Many of your routine decisions will have implications
for both the short- and long-term future, making your
high-wire act a bit easier.

2. *Position determines priority.* If you occupy a low- to
mid-level leadership position, Priority 1 includes your
basic job responsibilities, impending deadlines, and
emergencies—the operational tactics that keep the
business chugging along. Priority 2 consists of "someday" items that aren't urgent but will improve the team
and organization—things you can tackle when you
have time. When you rise to the upper rungs of the organizational ladder, your Priority 1 and Priority 2 tasks
flip-flop. Long-term strategy rather than day-to-day
tactics becomes ascendant. Spend most if not all your
time determining and communicating strategic priority
and direction, leaving the operational functions to subordinates.

3. *What does your leader expect?* Even if you occupy
a low rung on the leadership ladder, your superior(s)
may require your input on long-term strategy, either as
part of their due diligence or while grooming you for
a higher position. Or they may directly structure your
schedule, so you have little or no say about what to prioritize. Either way, grin and bear it.

4. *Necessity.* Does your team's workflow move in fits and
starts? Has it broken down? Even if you believe you
should focus on strategy, immediate needs may trump
long-term requirements. Don't ignore the squeals,
boings, and crashes because you've fallen behind on

next year's budget—or said budget may become a moot point. Similarly, if you're zipping along at 90 miles an hour but have no clue about your direction, stop long enough to consult with the policymakers. And if they have no clue either, grab the wheel until they can take over.

Unless you own a small business, you'll rarely need to consider strategy and tactics on an equal footing. While your job as a leader is to be a strategic enabler for the talents of both your subordinates and superiors, what you focus on depends primarily on your position. Middle managers rarely decide the company's direction; they make sure their teams get the product out on time and within budget. Similarly, the CEO can't be out in Cubeville cheering on the programmers instead of setting goals for the whole company—except on the occasional MBWA outing.

That's not to say the CEO should be ignorant of operational tactics. Nor should middle managers be ignorant of overall strategic goals. Both should know the basics up and down the chain of command, so they can do their jobs better. But inevitably, each will spend more time on one than the other, according to their place in the hierarchy. To the manager, too much strategic thinking represents a luxury; to the CEO, handling the daily operations is a waste of valuable, expensive time.

A Real-World Example

Roger Blythe explained how this works in his company, Chick-fil-A.

> We're very serious about the planning process, because we know it's so critical. It sets the direction for the work that we expect to accomplish during the next year.

In the context of strategic direction, one of the key roles of leadership is to get your associates or team members to come up with a plan to accomplish your overall objectives. Leaders aren't dictating to them; we have a very participative planning style. We make clear what the goals are and what the objectives are, but we give ownership of particular key buckets of work to individuals. Sometimes we use the term "thought leader" for key ideas and ask people to group thought leaders around a particular subject matter. Then each group has a scorecard once the goals are clearly laid out. The scorecard is updated monthly for me and my three key leaders, which holds us accountable through our performance management and evaluation.

MAKE ACCOUNTABILITY YOUR TOUCHSTONE

Whatever happened to accountability? Shortly after the Enron fiasco more than a decade ago, I happened across a cartoon that brought home corporate America's take on accountability (at least as far as the general public was concerned). It showed an angry-looking man in a suit bursting through a door labeled "Department of Accountability," only to find the tiny room beyond empty—because the single occupant was cowering beneath his desk.

That cartoon has stayed with me all this time, and it pops into my mind every time someone brings up the concept of accountability, which, sadly, seems to be less important than it used to be. The fact that the term "plausible deniability" even exists says it all, I think. People hide behind due diligence to avoid finger-pointing. Scapegoating has become common, to the point where it seems that some people could probably make a decent living by hiring themselves out to take the blame when things go wrong.

Nothing—*nothing*—substitutes for good, old-fashioned

accountability. That means holding everyone who works for you accountable for his or her actions. But here's the thing: as leader, the ultimate responsibility for everything that happens—bad, good, and indifferent—lands on *your* shoulders. It's one of the reasons they pay you the big bucks. You got your position by proving your ability to both lead and produce. As such, you can't squirm out of responsibility when it all goes pear-shaped (as my British colleagues like to say), though some folks certainly do try, don't they?

In a robust organization, accountability *must* represent part of the foundation of your leadership strategy—a touchstone that supports and informs everything you do. As team leader, you may not be at fault for everything, but you're still responsible. In the workaday vernacular, certain things "roll downhill" and they fetch up on your doorstep.

While you should hold team members who have erred accountable for their actions, you're still accountable for how the situation turns out. This may require you and everyone else to work harder to fix the problem. Or you may need to root out the rot altogether and replace the team members at fault with others who are more amenable to reason. As the late Stephen R. Covey once pointed out, "Accountability breeds response-ability."

While that statement seems glib at first glance, it actually hits the nail on the head. Accountability is valuable in a number of senses. When people make mistakes, they should accept responsibility and be held accountable. It helps them grow as individuals and team players alike. Sadly, several factors undermine this idea, not least the fact that high-ranking executives often successfully duck their responsibility for bad decisions even as lower-echelon employees receive harsh punishments for lesser transgressions. As a result, they learn to hide their errors, point fingers at others, or simply refuse to make decisions.

As I've pointed out previously, all business is a calculated risk. Thus, a non-punitive learning culture works best here. Just as you wouldn't expel a fourth-grader for failing a spelling test, the company mustn't fire someone for making a genuine error of judgment. That means allowing employees to fail forward and learn from their mistakes—or there will be no accountability at all.

And there *must* be accountability. It's a force that keeps us on the straight and narrow. Ultimately, we reap what we sow, which means it's a better idea to sow gold dust than rotten little excuses.

Not all your decisions will work out; in fact, some will come back to haunt you. But that doesn't mean you should shirk responsibility when something goes wrong, even if one of your people was wholly at fault, or the economy shifted unexpectedly and dumped you on your backside. You should have been paying closer attention.

When Accountability and Cross-Functionality Collide

Accountability also means it's up to you to communicate effectively outside your group. Here's how Roger Blythe describes the Chick-fil-A way:

> If we have interdependence with another group, such as Information Technology, we identify those interdependencies in the planning process. It's not enough to add the work in *our* plan; we have to make sure it's in *their* plan too. If it doesn't get into their plan, then there's no need for us to work on it. Sometimes, we're on the receiving end of that.
>
> For example, one of our roles is to evaluate most of the tests that take place at Chick-fil-A. We do our best to reach out into functional areas and try to understand what tests are planned for the year, but we still don't end up knowing all of them. We may get to the middle of the year only to discover a significant intervention or test is planned that, for whatever reason, we didn't know about. There's still the expectation

we're going to weigh it in, so we just have to adapt and be flexible enough to integrate it into our plans.

It's not all going to get done. We have to have conversations and be very comfortable about what priorities we are abandoning in favor of others. But at least we know what "nice to do" activities can fall off the list.

SLAY THE DRAGON OF COMPLACENCY

Few things can kill an organization more effectively than a false sense of security. Thus, always hope for the best but plan for the worst you can imagine. I assure you that, as friendly as we Americans are with the nations of Canada and the United Kingdom, somewhere in the bowels of the Pentagon are plans for how we'd react if those countries invaded us—not to mention plans for how we'd go about invading them. Paranoid? Maybe, but foreign relations can change overnight, and military planners have no choice but to take all conceivable futures into account.

What about things you can't plan for because you just can't conceive of them—like the February 2013 meteor explosion over Chelyabinsk, Russia? For such cases, you've got to develop your improvisational skills. I recommend you also solicit external suggestions when necessary, and never dismiss anything out of hand—because you may be too close to the situation to see the forest for the trees.

Eternal optimism serves you well in business, but only when you temper it with realism. Naturally things go wrong, so again, expect the best but plan for the worst. If you lack decent contingency planning right now, start hammering out the basics of Plans B, C, and D for every conceivable crisis. Don't delve too deep, lest you get paralyzed by too much analysis. But know what to do in case of a fire, flood, tornado, hurricane, blizzard, earthquake, terrorism, and even war. Respond as soon as possible no matter what happens, so you can protect your income stream, preserve jobs, and ensure your company's survival. Otherwise, one negative event could drop you into a pit from which you may never escape.

NO GUFF ALLOWED

The most profoundly unhelpful phrase in modern business consists of only four syllables: "That's not my job."

While uttering this phrase is rarely grounds for dismissal, maybe it should be. Job descriptions tend to be fluid nowadays, given the shifting challenges we face. In any case, the new task may not even have existed when you or Human Resources wrote the description for a particular position. But someone has to take it on in these days of doing more with less. So assuming that what you've instructed someone to do isn't dangerous, illegal, or unethical, you can't afford to accept this excuse from a team member.

To paraphrase Ben Franklin, you must hang together, or you'll surely hang separately. Even one person who refuses to do what you need done can damage a team's productivity. But human beings can be remarkably selfish, so you'll likely hear some variation of this excuse eventually. How should you handle it when you do?

Realize that legitimate excuses for declining a job *do* exist—especially the dangerous/illegal/unethical triumvirate I've already mentioned. So if you hear those dreaded words, look to the root of the problem.

Starting with the worst, here are four common objections and ways to counter them.

1. *It's beneath my dignity.* Nonsense! This is just another way of saying "I don't wanna." There's no shame in legitimate work if it's safe and doable. So tell them to step up or step out—that is, out the door. While this may seem like a harsh attitude, you don't have time to deal with prima donnas.

2. *I'm overqualified.* Maybe so, but sometimes you have to take one for the team—especially when the work you normally do has become scarce. I know an archaeologist who, when laid off at one company, got a new job the very same day because he was a known quantity and willing to do whatever needed to be done. His new company had little archaeological work at the time, but it did have a lucrative subcontract helping a multinational corporation clean up a Superfund site. The employers told him he might have to work with the Superfund team for a while, and in fact he did. Because he was willing to do so, he kept his job until the archaeological division got past its rough patch, and he was able to return to his chosen profession. The special training they gave him proved handy later on (which brings up the next, more legitimate complaint).

3. *I don't feel qualified/I don't have the training.* Clearly, you as the manager feel otherwise, or you wouldn't have chosen that team member for the task. Look more closely at the person's abilities. If he or she *isn't* qualified, rectify the situation. It may cost a little, but remember this: only ROI matters. If profits exceed costs, then you've done well.

4. *I don't have time.* This may also be true. If chosen team members feel overwhelmed, step in to help them prioritize, triage their task lists, eliminate time wasters, and make a hole for the new task—as long as it doesn't replace a task equally or more important. If they really do lack the time, you can legitimately assign the task to someone else.

In today's perilous business environment, we *all* have an obligation to pitch in to ensure team and organizational productivity—if only because making a sincere effort to contribute is the easiest way to keep your job.

So within certain broad boundaries, even when asked to do something not in their job descriptions, team members should be willing to do that new task. Remind them that it's necessary and make new hires aware of it in advance as you build your team.

CONQUER CRISES

As much as you try to structure your work time, there's no scheduling the unexpected. Emergencies and other crises can overwhelm you occasionally; no one has ever invented a predictive model (or crystal ball) that warns about everything that might blindside people during the average business day.

In a perfect world, we *would* expect the unexpected, since experience tells us how quickly things can go south. But somehow it rarely works out that way. Ever the optimists, most people look forward to a smooth workday proceeding according to plan and perfectly aligned with corporate goals. We blithely assume we can always keep to our schedules and maximize our productivity.

Optimism has its good points, but sometimes we let a positive, can-do attitude blind us to the reality that things can and do go wrong.

Certainly, planning can mitigate some disruptions. But that assumes you really can plan for them. Human beings have a perverse talent for inventing new problems for themselves. But when something comes completely out of left field, you have no choice but to fall back on good, old-fashioned flexibility. That means you deal with the disruptions as they appear, doing whatever you can to alleviate their effects without derailing your team's productivity.

If you're lucky, you can hand the problem off to someone else who can solve it more efficiently than you can. In other cases, it's best to take a direct hand, stepping in and mitigating the damage, so similar disruptions can't happen again.

Whatever the case, the real test of a work process isn't how well it works when everything's going smoothly, but how well it performs when you're slammed with unscheduled events. So let's look at ways to mitigate these events so you can keep your productivity on an even keel without killing yourself with overwork.

Pre-Crisis Planning

Even when all seems right with the world, you sometimes have to stop and take a good look around. A broad view will give you a better chance of seeing things as they come over the horizon. True productivity requires more than focus, drive, and determination; it also means putting systems and processes in place to monitor your workflow and safeguard it when things go awry.

I suggest establishing guidelines to direct your responses to various categories of emergencies—from unexpected tasks added suddenly to your team's to-do list to more serious threats like fires and natural disasters. If company-wide crisis-management plans already exist, review them thoroughly and don't hesitate to tweak or even replace them as necessary. If they don't exist, then step forward and propose them. The time you invest will eventually pay off.

In addition to your own ideas, consider the crisis planning practiced by aid organizations like the Red Cross and the Federal Emergency Management Agency (FEMA). How do they hold themselves in a state of readiness? What are their guidelines for specific disasters, and how can you adapt them to your needs?

You or a consultant could also perform vulnerability audits, which dissect in detail the processes and systems that make up a personal, team, or organization-wide workflow. These also identify potential weaknesses that might either cause or contribute to a crisis.[15] Large companies typically use such audits to pinpoint the worst potential problems, especially those associated with employee discontent.

You can adapt the concept to almost any type of emergent situation. For instance, a vulnerability audit might help you identify a productivity bottleneck that develops into a real issue only when a rush job forces your team to work faster than normal, or might illustrate how things would fall apart if a water main happened to flood your office. Once you know what can go wrong, you can plan for it.

Embrace Flexibility

You can also give your team elbow room by padding your schedule with a little slack time. Do so within the constraints of the existing schedule and take care not to overdo it; simply make sure your team's to-do list has enough flexibility to accommodate a bit of the unexpected. This doesn't mean you have to add empty slots to the schedule just in case, although that's an option. If you go that route and nothing comes up, then you can get extra work done on something else—or let everyone go home a bit early.

It may be wiser, however, to start separating your leadership to-do list into "Want to Do" and "Must Do" categories. Make sure that some of the lower-priority tasks on your list have some give in them, so you can reprioritize or postpone them at a moment's notice in favor of handling something unexpected. Then you're not wearing yourself and your team to a frazzle by adding more tasks to an already unwieldy schedule.

Handling a Crisis

When an unexpected event does occur, face the situation calmly. Most people either freeze in place, letting everything grind to a halt, or overreact in some way, making things worse. Neither paralysis nor freaking out can help your team. Instead, carefully and deliberately assess the situation, and then do whatever you must to fix it.

It helps to reframe the crisis as a challenge—something you can turn into an advantage somehow. That may make it easier to handle, at least in the short run. Even if you can't work the crisis into an advantage, you may all learn something from it, so be open to that possibility as you swing into action.

And speaking of action: motion beats meditation—as long as you and your team have enough facts to make an informed decision. Don't go off half-cocked. Unless you're dealing with something obviously dangerous like a life-threatening injury or an earthquake, reacting too soon may prove as disastrous as reacting too late.

Deciding how to react on the spur of the moment can be just as difficult, especially when dealing with a situation you haven't planned for.

In such a case, metacognition—thinking about how you think—can supply a solution. Even if you lack a crisis management or contingency plan for a particular conundrum, you can train yourself to think in such a way that you quickly decode the issue and invent a new plan on the spot.

Many business schools teach students to use a variation of the SLLR method in crisis situations. SLLR stands for the four common-sense steps involved: Stop, Look, Listen, and Respond. These strictures gain particular importance when the lines of communication, command, and responsibility have broken down.

So if you have no idea what to do when a disruption

rears its ugly head, *Stop*. Instead of reacting instinctively (or, worse, panicking), take a moment to cool down and think. Assess the situation, absorbing as much information as possible, *Look* at the obvious factors, and *Listen* to the people involved so you can learn more. After you have all the facts in hand (or at least as many as you can effectively gather), *Respond*. Move forward decisively and untangle the snarl.

If the problem takes the form of a bottleneck, then try to unplug it or find a way around it. In the average office, most personnel-related crises trace back to only a few people whose lack of preparation or consideration for others—or sheer orneriness in some cases—jams the gears of progress.

Some crisis creators may respond to reason if their obstructions are accidental or caused by a process flaw or missing resource. Often, you can handle them by lending a hand and providing what they need. Other crisis creators are themselves the root of the problem; they may delight in making life difficult for their coworkers. It doesn't matter why they do it; you simply have to find a (legal) way to deal with the problem.

The biggest crisis creator in your office may be in management. I've lost count of the number of times people have told me about bosses who consider every task top priority. The boss dumps tasks into their subordinates' in-boxes without pointing out which is the most urgent. If you find yourself faced with such a situation, take the bull by the horns and ask your manager the priority order for your tasks.

Involving Others

By the time you respond to a crisis, you should know whether you can deal with it alone. Never hesitate to seek assistance whenever you need it: one aspect of wisdom is knowing when to ask for help. Pull your team together before you implement your response and then split the issue into more easily handled sub-issues and parcel them out. Make sure everyone knows precisely what to do to solve his or her assigned piece of the problem.

If nothing else, ask for buy-in from the key players in the crisis, assuming you have the time to do so. As you implement your response, do what you can to keep everyone in the loop—including your clients or end users, if necessary. You may find the latter particularly important if you're a solo entrepreneur facing a crisis that stops you in your tracks, like a nasty case of the flu. In most cases, clients will respond positively to a request for a little extra time. If they don't, have a contingency plan in place so you can hand over work to a contractor during the down time.

Postmortem Dissection

After the crisis has passed and all the repercussions have died down, take time to dissect what happened. That way you'll know how to respond if it ever happens again. This amounts to more than Monday-morning quarterbacking. To quote philosopher George Santayana, "Those who forget history are doomed to repeat it."

Consider the types of investigations conducted by the National Transportation Safety Board (NTSB) for major accidents like airplane and train crashes. They take all the time necessary to carefully piece together the evidence and attempt to understand what happened, so a similar event can be avoided in the future. You may not have the time or resources of an organization like the NTSB, but you can modify its postmortem investigative style for your needs.

If possible, pull together the key people involved in the crisis, analyze what went wrong, and figure out how to keep it from recurring. If you lack the authority to call everyone together, conduct the postmortem on your own. This may require additional resources or a resource reallocation to pull it off, and, yes, it may take time you'd rather spend on something else. But in the long run, every second and cent you spend will be worth the cost if you can keep similar disruptions from shooting holes in your future productivity.

Cautious Optimism

It's human nature to be hopeful, and thank goodness; this gives us the drive to survive through thick and thin. But truly successful people refuse to let their guard down, no matter how positive their attitude. They understand the need for both careful preparation and superb flexibility.

Have contingency plans in place for everything you can think of, so you can roll with the punches as they occur— even when they come from unforeseen directions and take unanticipated forms. Most disruptions yield to a healthy dose of discipline and creative thinking. Once the crisis passes, you can analyze what happened and put plans in place to head off similar occurrences.

When faced with the unexpected, don't surrender to despair. Step forward, take charge, and, no matter how hard a crisis hits you, learn something from the situation. Better yet, find a way to profit from that knowledge. When life hands you lemons, don't just make lemonade. Find a way to sell that lemonade for a tidy profit, and then make lemon zest from the peels and plant the seeds for the future!

THE FINAL WORD

Once you've achieved buy-in, set goals, and made efforts to align those goals with your organization, you have to decide how to get there and what to do when you wander off-course. If the actual destination changes (which can happen during a corporate reorganization or reassessment of priorities), be prepared to plot a new course.

Accountability is the linchpin here; it links all of you at all levels, helping your people take serious ownership of their jobs while you exercise the ultimate responsibility. It's a heavy load, falling mostly on your shoulders. Yet everyone in the team must shoulder the load if we expect to be anything more than company hacks and salaried drones working toward the weekend in the short term, and retirement in the long.

Step forward, take up the challenge, and use it to carve your own niche out of the business jungle in your own inimitable style. Let your people do the same, within the broad guidelines you set.

With enough effort and the right tools, you can eventually build a voluntary culture of accountability in which you don't have to ride people to get them to do the right things at the right times. Then you can execute your strategy instinctively, no matter what happens.

Remember, no battle plan survives contact with the enemy. Whatever happens, you and your crew must be ready, willing, and allowed to adapt on the fly.

Drive

D

DRIVE

Leadership Role
Bulldozer:
Knock It Down

*Development
Opportunity*
Speed/Agility

As a leader, your greatest importance may lie in clearing the way forward for your team members. This typically involves smoothing out the speed bumps and removing any obstacles that block task execution, particularly the procedural ones. Think of yourself as a bulldozer, or, better yet, as a lineman on a football team protecting the ball carrier as he advances.

In a workplace context, you might guard your people from bureaucratic red tape by taking it on yourself, while making sure they have sufficient resources and facilities to get their work done. Your team must drive, push, move, and speed toward the goal with a sense of urgency. You're there to help them maintain the momentum.

Small businesses often have an easier time keeping momentum going than large corporations. The reason is simple: momentum is about growth and the ability to move forward. Smaller businesses can move more quickly, like speedboats; large organizations resemble cruise ships, and are harder to turn on a dime.

As a leader in a large organization, you might have encountered obstacles or tremendous setbacks in the past. If you feel defeated or frustrated, it might be difficult to remain passionate, forward-looking, and hopeful. That's when building momentum feels like just one more thing you have to do. And that's when, instead of embodying momentum, you see obstacles instead.

How can you eliminate whatever flies in the face of momentum and your team's forward drive? How much faster would your team be if they:

- Learned how to handle e-mail more efficiently?

- Found more time to think strategically?

- Weren't distracted by technology?

- Didn't spend so much time in meetings?

- Stopped being interrupted so frequently?

- Prioritized tasks better and stopped being reactive?

You be the judge—and the bulldozer.

Remove Obstacles from the Path 10

As it relates to a system or machine, efficiency is defined as "achieving maximum productivity with minimum wasted effort or expense." As it relates to people in the workplace, it's achieving "maximum results in minimum time," which is the trademark and tagline of my firm, The Productivity Pro, Inc.

Time is the most costly component of human capital. One employee who works an eight-hour day can be far more efficient and no less productive than another who works a twelve-hour day. What's the difference between these two? There could be many factors involved: intelligence, training, experience, willingness to work hard, or a penchant to focus. Whatever the case, in terms of efficiency, one person can get more work done in less time. How do you drive greater efficiency?

One way to make everyone speed up is for you, the leader, to discover and eliminate any obstacles that prevent team members from moving quickly. As an experienced professional, you already have the proper mindset in place.

Tinkering with the system, replacing old parts, and occasionally performing an overhaul to the workflow should be second nature by now. Strategic alignment simply represents a more generalized form of the same approach.

INSTILL THE NEED FOR SPEED

For decades, our culture has scrambled to keep pace with technological change. Companies have been ramping up their productivity to startling levels, helping to further advance technology that leads to greater productivity, and so on.

You can't compete effectively in the current marketplace without an agile internal culture capable of reducing time-to-market and cycle speed for all essential processes. If you don't put the pedal to the metal, the go-getters will leave you eating their dust.

How, then, do you build and maintain a culture of speed in your organization? Let's look at four basic principles.

1. *Perfect your systems.* Create and document procedures for every single task handled by your team, even those you consider minor. Make sure everyone who's involved learns them. Provide them with the right training or tools they need to do so. My office manager keeps a "white notebook" documenting every process she touches. If she gets hit by a bus tomorrow (heaven forbid!), I can hire a temp to step in and take over her job, thanks to her step-by-step instructions, and we won't be dead in the water. If you lose a key person, how fast can you be up and running? Consistently update your written procedures to match current reality, so nothing is out of date.

2. *Establish a broad support base.* Acquire buy-in from all team members. Provide them with target figures,

updated regularly. Motivate them in every way you can think of. Keep careful track of performance, rewarding fast, effective employees and thereby providing benchmarks for everyone else to shoot for. Spread the authority, so the workflow process doesn't break down because someone's on vacation, feels hesitant, or isn't allowed to make decisions. Do your best to keep everyone on the same page about productivity and minimize resistance wherever possible.

3. *Eliminate myopia.* When working closely with other teams, develop intergroup protocols to smooth the way. Include protocols to:

- Share data and information before starting new initiatives to avoid any duplication of effort.

- Establish rules for meetings, including who facilitates the meetings and records the minutes.

- Appoint specific individuals to act as go-betweens on certain topics between teams.

- Determine how you can leverage each other's resources and personnel.

- Keep your relationship flexible and forgiving.

   Encouraging speedy implementation may require delicate diplomacy, so strive to build bridges in all directions and on all levels—even as you aim to demolish information silos caused by inertia, greed, and misunderstandings.

4. *Communicate effectively.* Every person on your team must fully understand the organization's values, mission and vision, and strategic priorities, as well as

his or her place within that framework. Make it clear to people that they are advancing the entire organization, and explain how. Make sure everyone understands his or her job description down to the last comma. Take pains to clarify your directives, and tell employees *why* they need to follow through. Provide feedback quickly when someone requires you to do so. Tell people specifically what you need and when you need it. Let them ask questions when they need to. Similarly, ask others questions to ensure you understand what's being asked of you. It's always better to question someone until you understand than to do the job wrong.

Supercharge everything, from hiring and decision making to performance evaluation and product testing. Either you maintain your speed or you stagnate. When properly handled, a speed culture can both translate into and support the innovation necessary for an organization to remain flexible and relevant.

If you can't move your entire organization toward greater speed, then at least keep your piece of it driving forward.

LEAN AND MEAN MAKES GREEN

The concept of waste reduction has always been a part of American business tradition. We've taken Ben Franklin's common-sense reminders of "waste not, want not" and "a penny saved is a penny earned" to heart. Buying into this concept are such luminaries as Henry Ford, who introduced the modern assembly line, and Frank Gilbreth, Sr., and Frederick Winslow Taylor, the founders of time-and-motion studies and scientific management.

By the 1970s, Japanese industrial engineers had integrated these concepts and more into a framework dubbed "lean manufacturing" or simply "lean." In this parlance, anything that doesn't increase value for the customer is a waste.

It's easy to see how you can generalize this mindset to any systematic business process, as you define and target waste in defects, downtime, inventory, and underutilized resources. Systematic elimination of these wastes can result in faster processes, lower costs, higher quality, happier workers, and, most important, better results for your customers.

The point is to recognize these problems in your organization and develop a thorough understanding of them, so you can take corrective actions to limit them. Being human, we'll never eliminate waste completely; however, an organization that can trim away most of the fat will be more agile and more capable of competing in any marketplace. This allows for a saner workplace, in which productivity and profitability can rise to remarkable levels.

MAKE A DECISION ALREADY!

One big time waster you must work to trim is slow decision making. The ability to consistently make speedy decisions lies at the heart of any productivity initiative, especially if it affects an entire team or organization.

Those of us concerned with maximizing positive outcomes have invented a variety of guidelines to help people make solid, fast decisions. Some experts argue that all decisions deserve careful consideration and consensus building before they're implemented. I disagree, because this results in a slow, deliberate decision-making process and culture. Granted, for critical, strategic decisions with high stakes or financial impact, you certainly should take more time. But for average day-to-day issues, it's best to make relatively quick decisions.

Of course, no single decision-making method has a lock on perfection. You'll make mistakes occasionally, and some may prove costly. But don't let the possibility of a negative outcome stop you. Most of your decisions will be beneficial or will have few (if any) negative effects on your team.

Seconds Count

My father taught me from an early age that slow decision making can murder your momentum. That's especially true during opportunity and crisis situations as they develop. In his branch of the service, fighter pilots learn the OODA formula for engaging enemy pilots: Observe, Orient, Decide, and Act. Often a pilot has mere seconds to run through this process, because his opponent is appraising him the same way, just as quickly.

To shoot down your problems fast, develop your own accelerated thought processes as a way to maintain your momentum. You may not be as constrained in terms of time as a fighter pilot, but you can still hone your decision-making SPEED this way:

1. *Stop* long enough to gather the intelligence you need to get a handle on the issue.

2. *Ponder* what the issue means for your team. If it won't affect you at all, stop here.

3. *Educate* yourself on the issue as quickly as possible if it does have an impact or consequences.

4. *Evaluate* what you've learned.

5. *Decide* your best course of action and implement it without delay.

The SPEED formula offers a happy medium between the careful deliberation of decision making by consensus and the snap decisions of OODA. You don't bog down in perfectionism, but you still have time to fix your missteps.

Speedy decision making requires agility, flexibility, and a careful eye toward strategic alignment within your organization. With a little practice, you'll soon make all your leadership decisions with admirable SPEED.

DIFFERENT DRUMMERS, MATCHING GOALS

Can working in an open office, engaging in brainstorming sessions, and contributing to a business team actually hurt your productivity?

Excellent question, because all of the above are common modern business practices. You've likely experienced them in team-building retreats, quality management sessions, and meeting after meeting. The idea is to meld people into an organic solutions machine that operates as a single, comfortable unit with the organization's goals constantly in mind.

Most collaborative efforts do increase workplace productivity. However, when taken too far, they can also devolve into something psychologists call "groupthink," which is a collective attitude in which the drive for consensus drowns out individual creativity.

People with less perceived power often stay silent in the face of assertive people who dominate the group. When this happens, the team loses the benefit of their ideas. Group discussions and decision-making processes may become circular and stale. Sometimes group members even lose the ability to consider entire categories of ideas. In extreme cases, they may even shun or punish innovators and dissenters.

That Slippery Slope

Every company has its own corporate culture, and it takes only a few assertive people to dominate it. Whether intended or not, this situation offers fertile ground for the development of groupthink. If it gets out of hand, people risk becoming stagnant clusters of team players and yes-people afraid to speak up and take initiative. Or they could become members of dynamic groups that head willy-nilly down the path of failure, led by the assertive few. The quiet majority toe the company line for fear of losing their jobs. In today's economy, the company can easily find replacements for their squeaky wheels.

In the business world, this attitude leads to slow death because it stifles innovation. Consider what happened to Apple when its board of directors forced out cofounder Steve Jobs in the 1980s. The organization quickly devolved into a typical corporate bureaucracy in which groupthink nearly ran the company into the ground. Only the rehiring of Jobs—and subsequent innovations like the iMac, iPod, iPhone, and iPad—saved Apple from becoming a footnote in business history.

Jobs, of course, was a special case. While he led by force of personality, he also had the wisdom to allow workers the freedom to be who they were, including introverts like cofounder Steve Wozniak. Wozniak's late nights spent alone in his garage resulted in the first commercially viable Apple computer. Though "the Woz" didn't work entirely alone, his ability to apply his individual creativity to the project without undue interference got Apple's foot in the door of the computing world in the first place.

Weed Out Groupthink

While you do need some structure in the workplace, weeding out groupthink is important. The loudest member of a team can unduly sway others, even when he or she is wrong. Find a way to allow team members to slip their contributions into a discussion, if only by running them past you first so that you can introduce them. Intel-style one-on-one weekly meetings, now common in the high-tech industry, may be a good alternative. In general meetings, specifically tell attendees not to slap down new ideas before they have time to mature.

A corporate culture that's wide open to creativity and the conditions conducive to it represents the best of all possible worlds. In this scenario, those who work best in solitude might have access to special rooms where they don't have to wear noise-canceling earphones just to think (Microsoft has such "quiet rooms"). If this proves unrealistic, telecommuting represents another option for those who cherish their creative solitude—though admittedly, not all workers can be productive in such an environment.

To paraphrase the poet John Donne, no one is an island in the modern workplace. Collaboration is both a reality and a necessity if a company wants to stay in business. However, when group culture morphs into groupthink, flexibility goes out the window. So leave room for the quiet to innovate and be heard, and your organization will have an easier time navigating the rapids of modern business.

DIVINE PERFECTION VS. HUMAN REALITY

Actor Michael J. Fox once said, "I am careful not to confuse excellence with perfection. Excellence I can reach for; perfection is God's business."

It's true that as your experience and skills evolve, you should occasionally push the envelope of your own and your team's constraints. But do you know your limitations? You can't always do everything perfectly.

It's important to have high standards for your teamwork;

indeed, you need them if you expect to achieve consistent productivity. But be aware of the difference between high standards and unrealistic expectations. When your standards for yourself and your team become so lofty they tick over into the irrational, then they'll simply slow you down. Maintaining absurdly high standards can be as bad as having no standards at all.

I don't offer this as an excuse to slow down or slack off. I advocate always striving for excellence. But at the same time, some things are good enough at 90 percent. If you try to consider every possible outcome and arrange for every contingency before making your first move, you may have trouble getting started at all. While some of us like to say we work best under pressure, that's rarely true. You're like the undergraduate scrambling at the eleventh hour, staying up all night to write a paper assigned months before. More often than not, the results reflect the amount of time spent on the task.

Rather than hold yourself to divine standards, be a REALIST:

1. *Recognize your limits.* No one knows you and your team better than you and your team. Break your task or project into manageable pieces and set solid deadlines for achieving each.

2. *Energize.* You know that you and your team are good at what you do or you wouldn't be where you are now. So get psyched up, individually and collectively, before you start any new projects.

3. *Acknowledge reality.* You and your people might make a few mistakes as you work on a task. You might even fail. Push past the fear of failure and don't let it stymie productivity.

4. *Leave perfectionism behind.* It only drags you down. Do the best you can; even compete with other teams if that motivates you. But don't expect perfection every time, because it's unnecessary. My French-Cajun grandmother used to say, "Don't waste time putting lipstick on a pig."

5. *Implement your plan.* Once you have all your ducks in a row, take a deep breath and dive in. Move. Take action.

6. *Seize the initiative.* No battle plan survives contact with the enemy. Even in the workplace, most situations prove chaotic; issues you never expected might suddenly appear on the horizon or in your face. Some may prove advantageous. When new opportunities for success present themselves, grab them quickly.

7. *Take your best shot at the unexpected.* Since you can't foresee every nook and cranny of the future, don't try. Make what preparations you can and handle the little things as they pop up.

Self-Honesty: The Best Policy

Don't equate a realistic assessment of your situation with pessimism. Realism represents a form of intellectual honesty, which trumps the gung-ho silliness that sometimes sweeps American business.

Yes, you can take reasonable precautions and gather as much data as possible before taking action. But don't let an obsessive need to get everything just right waste your time and energy. Once you've meditated long enough, it's time to put on your REALIST armor and leap into the fray.

THE FINAL WORD

All teams include someone who makes things easier for others to do their jobs. On a football team, blockers protect the quarterback and ball carriers. In the white-collar world, the team leader removes the obstacles, from crushing groupthink, to speeding up decision making, to being a REALIST rather than a perfectionist.

One of your primary titles today should be "Facilitator." But facilitation goes beyond dealing only with people and processes. Chapter 11 looks at both physical and technological ways to facilitate success.

Add Enablers to the Equation CHAPTER **11**

As a professional speaker, I occasionally get a question from an audience member that no one has ever asked me before, so I must think quickly on my feet. You may experience similar situations in your own career. Suppose you're the team expert on Boxlets, your company's proprietary spreadsheet program. If your manager needs a fact quickly or a doubtful customer grills you on why he should buy Boxlets and not Microsoft Excel, you need to think fast and produce accurate answers.

To get your brain to move as quickly as you need it to, here's what has helped me THINK faster:

1. *Take care of yourself.* This should always come first, but when time grows short, what usually takes the hit? Rest, diet, and exercise. How can you do your job well if you're dragging around on five hours of sleep or feeling sluggish from those twenty extra pounds? Stop holding yourself back. Get the right amount of sleep, eat decently, and exercise regularly, so your brain will

function at its best. That way, you can have last week's sales figures at the tip of your tongue.

2. *Hone your memory.* While rote memorization doesn't beat true learning, you do need to keep your facts immediately accessible. In any case, having a good memory helps in traditional learning, too. Study the important things repeatedly until you've internalized them. How many fields can Boxlets 3.0 handle? How many types of charts can it produce? How many megabytes of memory storage does it require? If you have memory problems, you can train yourself using memory enhancement techniques ranging from Dale Carnegie to the latest memory aid software. Keep trying them until you find something that fits your learning style.

3. *Improve your focus.* As I write this, I can hear the thudding bass of a car's music down the street. The driver must think the whole world wants to hear his playlist. Working in a standard open-plan office can prove even more challenging, with its hallway conversations, ringing phones, clattering keyboards, and whirring photocopiers. Such distractions subconsciously demand a piece of your attention and therefore slow your thinking. When you need to get in the zone, seek solitude in an empty conference room, work from home, or wear headphones and listen to classical music. Certainly turn off your e-mail, phone, and cell. How else can you beta-test Boxlets 4.0 undisturbed?

4. *Nourish your brain.* All Boxlets and no play makes you a dull expert. Almost everything you read teaches you something, so give your mind the "food" it needs. Read a lot. Learn new facts. Study a foreign language. Play

Sudoku. Sharpen your intellect with *New York Times* crossword puzzles. Keep your mind active, and you'll be able to jumpstart the synapses with minimal effort the next time someone asks you, "What version of Boxlets do you recommend for Ubuntu 13.47 on an IBM enterprise server?"

5. *Knowledge = Power.* It may be a cliché, but that doesn't make it wrong. Learn every bit of lore you can about your specialty and associated topics so you can reply with authority. Broaden your knowledge outside your own expertise as well. I used to tease my dad and call him the "Jack of all trades and master of none." This actually wasn't true, because he has a Ph.D. in philosophy and literally wrote the book the cadets at the Air Force Academy studied from. But he had "the gift of gab" (I suppose that's where I got it). He was so knowledgeable about so many things that he could talk intelligently to anyone about almost anything.

If you put the THINK formula into action, you may not have to think consciously when someone asks you a question; the answer will be there on the tip of your tongue. Even in a situation outside your immediate expertise, THINK holds you in good stead because it keeps you mentally agile, flexible, and resilient, which puts you light years ahead of most people.

TECHNOLOGICAL SUPERCHARGERS

Use improved technology to allow your workers to boost production. Janie Wade told me that Baylor's wonderful new technologies have allowed the health-care organization to streamline many systems that used to be manual. From the registration kiosks that allow tech-savvy patients to register themselves to the electronic routing of invoices that alleviates paper shuffling and lost invoices, technology has allowed Baylor to save money and be more efficient.

"Health care is moving into the age of the electronic health record, where clinicians can quickly access information about the patient," Janie said.

> Because the record is electronic, we can now query quality metrics that used to be collected through chart review. It's allowing us to direct resources *away* from data collection and *toward* data analysis. We can identify unnecessary variation in care that, when eliminated, can lead to better outcomes for the patient. Upon discharge, the patient's family physician can view the hospital record, understand what occurred in the hospital, and develop a plan of care that prevents readmission.

IMMENSE PRODUCTIVITY

No one doubts that more efficient communication has transformed modern business. No longer do organizations have to centralize in order to keep communications tight and the workflow responsive. Nor are they required to allow people in outlying offices a high level of self-rule while waiting for long-distance directives.

In this information era, we can relay instructions or ask and answer questions almost immediately. It began with the telegraph, followed by the telephone and fax. Today, we have immediate communication technologies like e-mail, texting, social media, and instant messaging, all of which can contribute to workplace productivity if handled wisely.

Acceptance has come more easily for some of these new technologies than for others. Take e-mail, which we've embraced so extensively that it now functions as the *de facto* communications hub in most offices. E-mail lets us knit together the entire world with little effort, often more cheaply than the telephone. Admittedly, nothing will replace the personal contact that speaking on the phone allows, especially since long-distance calls cost very little now. But unless you use Skype or a similar technology, you still have to fork over higher fees for calls to other countries, whereas e-mail to anywhere costs virtually nothing once you've set up Internet and intranet connections.

The same applies to instant messaging (IM). In my experience, the business world hasn't embraced IM as enthusiastically as e-mail at the management level, most likely because it's bad for concentration. However, individuals have been installing IM programs on their office computers for years, arguing that it's a huge productivity boon, because they don't have to wait for an e-mail response and it's less intrusive than phone calls.

Given its quick response time, IM does offer an excellent collaboration tool for distributed teams. A 2007 study conducted among forty-four workplace teams in the United States indicates that, in some circumstances, IM works better than e-mail for this purpose, yielding one extra idea per average than a comparable e-mail session.[16] Effective brainstorming requires you to throw open the filters and let all the ideas through, even those that seem dumb at first glance. Dumb or not, they may spark more reasonable ideas that you and your team can implement profitably. Indeed, IM moves too fast for over-judging new ideas. In contrast, when using e-mail we tend to filter our responses, killing off ideas before they're truly born.

Getting instant feedback through IM can also limit confusion, or at least reduce the time necessary to clarify directives.

Holy IMperfections, Batman!

Naturally, IM has its negative aspects. For example, it represents yet another external distraction for you to guard against. Having an IM dialog box pop up suddenly while you're working on something important can be annoying. But proponents say they find it easier to deal with a quick instant message than with a phone call, and they can more easily return to their primary task before they lose their train of thought. That said, you can always set your IM on "Do Not Disturb" when you're trying to focus, just as you can disable e-mail alerts and let your phone calls roll over to voice mail.

IM also allows plenty of potential for abuse, especially among those who feel obliged to keep in constant contact with people outside the office. This factor drives some of the resistance from managers. Also, spammers have invented ways to slip their ads into unregulated systems in the form of "spim." In addition, total strangers may contact you because your user name sounds interesting. While that may be part of the charm for recreational messaging, it doesn't fly in the workplace.

Fortunately, you can implement something like e-mail white-listing on most IM systems, allowing only messages from people on an approved list. IM systems with firewalls that work only within a company intranet have been on the market for years. These systems may be expensive compared to freebies like those offered by Yahoo, Google, and AOL, but they allow full company control of the resource while eliminating spim and outside entry. They also solve the problem of recording and storing instant messages for posterity; some even let you easily search logged messages, a problem that has plagued recreational IM users from the outset.

How does IM stack up to cell-phone texting? Well, with

instant messaging, you don't have to worry about Black-berry thumb (a repetitive strain injury caused by frequent use of the thumbs to press tiny buttons on cell phones, smartphones, etc.). And who wants to squint at that tiny little screen? Phone texting doesn't compare with instant messaging on a full-size monitor with a normal keyboard.

Here to Stay

E-mail will probably remain the king of office communication for the foreseeable future (at least to receive a notification that you have a message in a social media network). It certainly allows a reasoned discourse that gives you time to organize your thoughts before replying. Still, IM allows a faster, freer flow of ideas, making it valid as a productivity resource, particularly when brainstorming or performing online customer service. So it has a place in the office as a valid productivity tool. IM will probably stay until we invent something better—like direct brain-to-brain communication.

AIRPLANES?
WE DON'T NEED NO STINKIN' AIRPLANES!

Your marketing team is in Chicago; you work from your office in Denver; and the team works from field sites all over the globe. You need to connect voice-to-voice to discuss next quarter's sales efforts and don't have the budget to travel to a central location. Teleconferencing to the rescue!

Conference and video calls can be a great way to connect virtual teams from around the world. They're less expensive than face-to-face meetings, often take less time, and allow teams to communicate more informally, ask questions, and solve problems better than e-mail.

Holding a teleconference should be a no-brainer. What's

so hard about a group of.people talking on the phone? All you have to do is connect everyone and make decisions as if you were in person, right? Well, no. That's the dilemma. This isn't your normal phone call. Instead, think of a tele-conference as a meeting. It's especially complex if some participants are meeting face-to-face while others are re-mote, which is a common occurrence. To pull it off, you'll have to prepare for it in the same way you would a meeting, with a few extra details.

To ensure the success of your next teleconference, fol-low the three Ps of effective teleconferencing—planning, process, and protocol.

Planning

Planning involves whatever you do to get ready for the tele-conference—and remember, you must prepare for it like any other meeting. Include the following items in your planning:

- Because you're coordinating the calendars of several busy people, scheduling a teleconference can take days. Give yourself at least a week before the desired meeting day to find a time convenient for all.

- A teleconference can become unmanageable with more than ten people, so limit the number of participants to those whose presence is truly required. Include people who can make a significant contribution to the discussion and copy people who need to know what's happening in the minutes following the call.

- One week before the meeting, solicit input for items to add to the agenda. Send a detailed meeting agenda at least two days ahead of the call, specifying the meeting's objective and required decisions. Don't forget to send all documents, notes, and pre-work or reading required in good time. Keep the process simple and the schedule short. Most people can't pay attention while listening and looking out into space for more than about 30 minutes. If you have more issues to discuss than time available, plan several teleconferences to discuss different objectives.

- Include the teleconference phone number and PIN number with the e-mail messages one week before, two days before, and the day of the meeting.

- Test the teleconferencing equipment several days before the actual meeting. Conduct a few trial runs with the other locations to ensure you can hear people and they you. Dealing with surprises on the day of the meeting is no fun as frustrated participants sit around while you troubleshoot the equipment.

Process

Process addresses what to do to conduct an effective teleconference *during* the meeting.

- The person who calls the meeting can act as the "voice traffic controller," or another person may be appointed as the facilitator. This person keeps the discussion moving and on track, noting topics to discuss based on a timed agenda and asking specific people to report.

- Before you speak, remember that some people may not recognize your voice. Even if you think "everyone knows me," always begin with your name—

"This is Laura"—and then speak. When you pick up the conversation again, repeat your name—"This is Laura again."

- Don't be afraid of silence. Because the phone is devoid of facial expressions, you can't always read emotion. Someone may be formulating a question in his or her mind and need another minute to chime in. Also, realize that silence doesn't always imply consent.

- Make sure participants have finished speaking before you begin, or you'll interrupt them mid-sentence.

- If a group of people are meeting in the same room with other remote sites dialing in, make the virtual participants feel included. For example, if someone cracks a joke and the group bursts into laughter, let the others know who said what and repeat the joke.

Protocol

Points of protocol indicate rules of etiquette and engagement for participants to follow:

- Use the "mute" feature of the phone when you're not speaking, so participants can't hear your background music or your neighbor's barking dog. Some systems allow the facilitator to "mute all" participants, taking them off mute at selected times to ask or respond to questions.

- Be present. "I'm sorry, I wasn't paying attention; could you repeat the question?" is an all-too-common phrase heard during calls. Don't risk sounding unprofessional. Stay focused. As good as you think you are at multitasking, the conscious mind isn't capable of reading e-mail and listening to a speaker at the same time. Surfing the Internet or pressing the mute button so you can carry on another conversation effectively removes you from the meeting.

- Keep side conversations to a minimum. As a remote teleconference participant, it's frustrating to hear "babbling" in the background. More than that, it's difficult to distinguish the actual speaker from the other noise, and it often sounds like a constant echo on the line.

- Read all pre-work and be prepared to participate actively in the conversation. Just because others can't see you doesn't mean they won't miss your voice if you're silent.

Follow these 3 Ps and your teleconference should go off without a hitch—at least as far as any meeting ever does. The same rules apply to videoconferencing. Though not nearly as common as teleconferencing and face-to-face meetings, video meetings are the wave of the future. We'll see them become more common as technology improves and costs decrease.

Once telepresence rooms and 3-D conferences become mainstream, you'll never have to leave your office to appear at a conference table "in person" continents away. Communications technology has made enormous strides in the last century, and it's still growing by leaps and bounds.

LIKE A SURGEON

Too often, we waste time on activities that don't align with our corporate priorities, either from misguided efforts to try new things, or because we're still using legacy processes that should have been shut down years before.

Take a close look at what you're doing that might actually be detracting from your productivity and do what you can to eliminate the useless items. Push it hard and fast and get it done.

Janie Wade told me about an internal program called ABC Baylor that educates employees on rapid cycle improvement. It focuses multidisciplinary teams on a particular metric and gives them the tools to improve that metric within a short time. They require all managers to go through the program, and executives are obligated to sponsor several initiatives each year.

Similarly, Roger Blythe of Chick-fil-A told me a fascinating story about purposefully abandoning tasks that aren't in alignment with priorities. He said,

> For many years, we've talked about the need to include whitespace within our plan. In other words, don't plan every single hour of every single day for the next year. So this year, we did something very simple—we created a distinction between tasks that *must* be done versus tasks that would be *nice* to do. We made sure at the individual project and task level that team members had a clear understanding of both—critical and secondary. Then we left enough room on the calendar for the issues that just come up. When the unexpected occurs, leaders have to make a judgment call about which work is more important—is it this or what we already said had to be done? And is it even more important than other work we've already identified that would be nice to do?

Don't Take on More Just to Turn a Buck

Every new task you put on your team's plate slows them down, because they can only spread their time, attention, and energy across so many efforts. Steven Gangwish of CSS Farms said,

> In terms of our strategy, the biggest change I've seen that our company has made is when we're thinking about a growth option. There are many opportunities coming at us on a regular basis, so we've tried to make a concerted effort to think about how each would affect our business. Does it have long-term enterprise value for our business, rather than just adding revenue or profit for one year? We only have so much time that our people can spend in any given day, any given year, and we had better be spending it on projects that can create the biggest bang for the buck.

CLEAR, CONCISE COMMUNICATION . . .
AND OTHER C-WORDS

Poor communication can absolutely wreck team productivity, especially if it depends on people knowing exactly what they need to do from moment to moment. Thus, relaying instructions and requests for new tasks, whether vertically or laterally within an organization, requires clear, concise communication between the participants.

Counting the Cost

The need for clear workplace communication may seem obvious at first glance, but common sense about communication isn't so common. Too often, requests or orders lack clarity, even at the most basic level; usually, they boil down to little more than "please get this done," without any details as to how and when.

Worse, many recipients of flawed communications are reluctant to ask for clarification. Sometimes they just don't want to irritate the requestor by pestering them for more information. In other instances, they don't care to invest the time required. Whatever the cause, they can end up climbing the wrong mountain, generating an avalanche of wasted effort and time. Failure results because they didn't want to bother someone—or simply didn't want to bother.

Compiling Your Capital

No doubt you've suffered the results of tangled communications at one point or another. I like to tell the story of a vice president I worked with at an automotive supply company. He asked an accountant for a ballpark estimate on something—an estimate he thought might take fifteen minutes to produce. The accountant spent ten hours coming up with a highly accurate estimate. Who was at fault for the waste of time? Both: the CEO for not making his assumptions clear, and the accountant for not asking for clarification.

The next time you need to relay a request or order to someone on your team, think about it first. Type it out and then edit it for maximum clarity. Mull over the structure of the message. Have you used jargon the recipient might not know? Have you couched it in vague or indefinite terms? Have you laid out a definite deadline? Did you employ passive phrases or weasel words like "if possible" or "when you can"? Perhaps the worst offender here is "ASAP." To one individual, ASAP might mean "drop everything and get it done now"; to another, it might mean "when you can get to it" or "once you've finished everything else." Be clear: What do you mean when you say ASAP?

You can't afford to make any of these mistakes. Take time to construct your communications as tightly as possible. Fancy or murky language can easily lead people down the wrong path, so don't use a five-dollar word when a one-cent one will do. Lay out specific expectations on deliverables in terms of timeline and quality. Certain assumptions (for example, specialized jargon) that work just fine with specific coworkers or subordinates may break down when applied to others. If they don't share a common frame of reference with you, you could leave them in the dark or lead them down the wrong path.

To raise your team and personal productivity, communicate completely and clearly with your coworkers, superiors, and subordinates. Doing so is especially crucial when you need something that's integral to maintaining your workflow.

Making your communication clear doesn't require much more time or effort, and the results invariably justify your investment. If you'll take a few minutes at the outset to make sure everyone involved has received and understood a communication properly, then you'll have a better chance of getting what you want.

THE FINAL WORD

If you want your team members to maximize their productivity and ability to execute in the moment, make the process easier by facilitating their technology and methodologies. You can take advantage of simple approaches like the THINK method as well as modern technology, such as instant messaging and teleconferencing. Just be sure to strike the proper balance; weigh the pros and cons of any new methodology, and be vigilant in its application.

Do your best to trim away anything that doesn't contribute to your execution, being careful about what you add to your team's plate. Look for long-term advantages, not short-term profits, and realize you'll have to remove something for everything you add, or you risk stress and overwork.

Finally, when communicating in the workplace, keep your phrasing and delivery as clear as possible to maximize productivity. Be assertive and straightforward; never hem and haw. Use simple language, avoiding jargon when you can. Immediately acknowledge any communications you receive, and get acknowledgment back from those you communicate with. Time is money, so waste as little of it as you can.

In this book's final chapter, let's look at common workplace time wasters and how we can root them out. The goal? To ensure you have more time to work on excellent strategic execution.

Eliminate Time Wasters

I'm a big country music fan, and I love this quote from Garth Brooks: "The greatest conflicts are not between two people, but between one person and himself."

Few people can honestly say they've never dragged their heels on a task or dawdled over a project they should have put more effort into. We may not feel proud about it, but we procrastinate anyway. Some people say it's because they work better under pressure. But usually it boils down to one of three common issues: feeling overwhelmed, fearing failure, or disliking the task.

Then, too, I've known people who dilly-dallied because they feared running out of work too soon. This happens most often in jobs that continue only as long as the work lasts, such as temporary positions (though it can happen in any workplace where the worker's future seems uncertain). Downsizing, right-sizing, and all the other euphemisms used to describe laying people off have encouraged this mindset.

My husband, John, was a letter carrier when I first met him (my paternal grandfather had a thirty-year career as a carrier, so of course I was enamored). He told me the carriers didn't go as fast as they were able to go, because their supervisors measured their delivery rate. As a carrier, if you proved you could deliver more mail than the bosses estimated you could, they just piled more on you, so then you had to go faster to keep up. In effect, they punished you for doing a good job. This resulted in more work and more exhaustion without more pay. Naturally, the carriers weren't as efficient as they could be. Can you blame them? The postal service was measuring and rewarding the wrong things. (No wonder it's in financial trouble.)

One day, a fellow came up to me after a speech and shared that at times he deliberately procrastinated. When I asked why, he said he was in a union, and he'd learned from experience that doing his work too quickly simply got him more and harder work. That resulted in both personal exhaustion and resentment from his coworkers because he "made them look bad." When he tried to cut back to normal working hours, his bosses treated him as though he was slacking off.

So you can see the logic in procrastinating sometimes. However, these examples represent the exceptions, not the rule. Here's the reality: Sometimes you and your people procrastinate no matter what. You know what you need to do, but you don't feel like doing it. You realize you're putting off certain tasks, but you keep choosing to do it anyway.

Typically, we procrastinate because we don't feel like doing what we know we should be doing, based on a simple lack of discipline. Bottom line: Procrastination wastes time. It's no less a time waster than excessive socializing, doing personal business at work, or overusing the Internet. Unlike those activities, though, procrastination doesn't always stand out as an obvious productivity drain; therefore, rooting it out mostly comes down to self-policing.

RESOURCEFUL SELF-DISTRACTION

Theodore Roosevelt, the twenty-sixth president of the United States, is reported to have said, "In a moment of decision, the best thing you can do is the right thing, the next best thing is the wrong thing, and the worst thing you can do is nothing."

So, if you're unable to work on the right thing, how about doing the next best thing? If you're going to procrastinate, at least try to do something productive. I call this Resourceful Self-Distraction, which I consider a lesser form of procrastination, because you're still *doing* something. On a scale of 1 to 5 (in which the worst thing you could tackle is a Sudoku puzzle and rates 1, while the best is your top priority of the day and rates 5), let's settle on something rated a 3. If you insist on procrastinating, how about distracting yourself with one of these resourceful tasks instead?

- Clean out a few files.

- Clear your e-mail in-box or the top of your desk.

- Transfer your attention to a medium-priority task.

- Make one of the important-but-not-urgent tasks on your Someday list a reality.

- Knock out a low-priority task such as delivering mail to a colleague, refilling your pop-up note dispenser, or watering your plant.

- Check in with those to whom you've delegated specific tasks but haven't heard back from.

- Take a brief walk to clear your head, vowing to get to work immediately when you return.

- Plan out a new project on a whiteboard.

You can also take an opportunity to visit your creative "third place." It might be Starbucks, the library, a hotel room you visit quarterly for a writing retreat (my favorite), or the gazebo in the garden. It might be something you do, like taking an early-morning walk. It might even be some combination of all of these. Being in this place can help clarify your strategic thinking.

SNEAKING IN PRODUCTIVITY

If you do even one of these things listed, you're not totally procrastinating: you're doing something sort of worthwhile instead of shooting yourself in the foot with complete time wasters. After crossing a less-important item off your list, you might find it easier to dive into your highest-priority task.

While I'm a big critic of staying busy just to stay busy (because it often doesn't equate with results), I do have to admit that tackling low-value items this way can act as a springboard to launch you into greater accomplishment. Sometimes you simply have to go with the task that fits your energy for the moment and gain some momentum. Once you get moving, you may find yourself on a roll doing a high-priority activity.

KNOW WHAT *NOT* TO DO

It happens every day: you finish a task, check it off your list, and feel a sense of accomplishment. Great, now what?

It's important to decide quickly what to do next. But it's equally important to decide what *not* to do next—and this applies as much to you as a leader as it does to your team. Each of you has to choose the appropriate course of action by design, not by default, to maximize your productivity as a unit.

Here are some considerations you and your team should *not* use to decide what to do next:

Based on what you feel like doing. Our emotions are usually poor judges of value. You may have something due tomorrow you absolutely hate to work on. But what other choice do you have? Instead of reorganizing the files on your hard drive, jump into the tough task immediately. That way, you won't have to worry about it anymore.

By the order in which tasks appear. E-mails in your in-box, messages on your voice mail, and tasks on your to-do list rarely appear in priority order. In a more general sense, don't open an e-mail and deal with it because it suddenly appeared in your box. When working on a critical task, don't answer the phone simply because it rings. When you're in a meeting, don't look at your phone because it buzzes. If you absolutely can't help checking these devices, then shut them off.

By who's screaming the loudest. Unless it's your boss and you will get fired otherwise, don't respond to other people's requests according to how loudly they demand your attention. Some people have a way of making everything seem like a crisis; they insist you make their tasks your top priority. If someone comes to you with a true emergency, certainly handle that first; otherwise, state when you'll be in touch or can handle the request. Let others know what to expect in terms of a deadline, while communicating with no uncertainty that you won't do it now.

By what comes to mind. Just because you think about an activity doesn't mean you should do it right then. The human brain often operates in a random manner, with your subconscious tossing up solutions or reminders as it comes up with them. If a sudden idea seems useful, write it down so you can come back to it. But don't chase the shiny object or work on the first thing you think about. Though you might feel busy and "in motion," you're probably creatively procrastinating.

By the order of the sticky note. Just because you've unearthed a sticky note from beneath a pile of reports or project files doesn't mean you need to get right on it. Weigh all the other factors first. If you haven't looked through that pile of paper in a year, chances are you can simply toss the note with no ramifications. If it had become an emergency, you would have known about it long before discovering it.

By questioning the right path to take. You face moments of truth several times a day. Don't spend more than a few seconds on them and don't open Facebook or play solitaire while you "decide." If you need a break, take one on purpose. Otherwise, pick a priority and go with it.

WHAT'S GOTTA COME NEXT?

Decide what to do next by order of priority. Clearly, you can't measure productivity by the number of items scratched off a list, because if you do, you may never get to the high-value activities at the bottom.

Adopt the battlefield concept of triage for task management. I thoroughly describe this schema in my book *What to Do When There's Too Much to Do*, so I won't repeat it in detail here. Basically, be willing to drop the lowest-priority items (the "nice to do" tasks) in favor of the top-priority "have to do" tasks. For example, suppose you must do twenty-one things as part of your job, and five are critical to the operation. You'd focus first on those top five and then work on the remaining sixteen items if you have time. If time runs short, those tasks roll to tomorrow. This is much more preferable than completing the sixteen minor tasks and leaving the top five undone.

As Carlos Amesquita, Director of North America Global Business Services at Procter & Gamble, pointed out,

> One way of handling that is working backward with the end in mind—what needs to be true for us to deliver it in, say, nine months. Start working backwards, and then you'll find your constraints. Some things take nine months to do; having a baby, for example. You really can't have it any earlier.
>
> You'll find those situations, and you'll find others where you'll say, "This step isn't needed." Or "Yes, I can do this if I put more people to work on this." Or "I can do things in parallel." There may be some efficiencies to be gained if you realize there's redundancy, or you could perhaps simplify or eliminate a step. If you set the constraints, the constraints will force you to weed what is unnecessary.

If you want to prosper, you can't choose what to do next based on how you feel or its position on your to-do list. Nor can you afford to check your bank balance or buy airline tickets for your next vacation while you put off getting started. That path leads to disorganization, feeling overwhelmed, and poor productivity. To get things done, discipline yourself to triage tasks as they arrive—because no one else will do it for you.

DO WE REALLY NEED THIRTY-TWO PEOPLE AT THIS MEETING?

According to American journalist George Will, "Football combines the two worst things about America: it is violence punctuated by committee meetings."

Indeed, meetings may be the bane of our workplace existence. I don't mean events like professional conferences, which generally represent valuable educational experiences. I refer to those self-proliferating time wasters that bring us together to discuss ways to maximize team productivity but accomplish the exact opposite. They seem to expand as time goes by, and when everyone has to have a say, meetings can drag on for hours, killing productive momentum.

Yet meetings remain absolutely necessary if teams expect to meet their strategic goals. The higher you rise in an organization, the more of your time you'll spend in meetings making decisions, determining strategic direction, and collaborating with other leaders. At their best, meetings help us share information, coordinate plans, ensure alignment, maximize limited resources, and spark innovation.

Squeezing in Some Productivity

To have a productive meeting, you first must know why you're meeting and then stick to the agenda you've set and limit attendance only to those who can contribute. For example, if you oversee the sales department and a meeting involves purchasing new software for the corporate accountants, you probably don't need to attend. On the other hand, accounting may need to attend your quarterly sales meetings if they track your department's costs or net profits.

Use these guidelines to decide how many people should attend your meeting, based on meeting type:

- *Communicating company strategy.* These all-hands meetings can include everyone in the organization, as long as the facilitators limit questions and stick to a strict schedule. These meetings often include speeches by thought leaders or subject matter experts.

- *Brainstorming.* Limit these sessions to twenty people maximum. Consider breakout sessions in which smaller subgroups handle specific topics and report in to the facilitator.

- *Problem solving/discussion.* It's best to have fewer than fifteen attendees. If you have more people who should participate, especially when company direction is involved, consider breaking into two or more meetings.

- *Action planning/alignment.* All participants should have a thorough understanding of the organization's strategic alignment and their place in it. Smaller is better, especially when seeking buy-in, so aim for fewer than ten attendees. That said, at least inform your entire group about your strategic goals. If you lead an especially large team, this feeds back to the first item.

- *Decision making.* Limit this meeting to the small group that the decision will directly affect.

Getting Real

Some people believe that anyone a meeting might possibly affect, even tangentially, should attend. Inoculate yourself against this idea. Otherwise, where will it end? You'll lose days of wasted time, and half the people who attend the meetings will either doze off or go catatonic before you finish.

When in doubt, don't invite people to meetings who need not attend. Don't attend meetings in which you and your people have no useful input. Some observers suggest kicking out the least valuable attendee anyhow. Apple's Steve Jobs always kept his meetings small when possible, and he wasn't averse to excusing people if he thought they didn't belong. You may want to do the same, while structuring the agenda so you can dismiss some of the attendees after they address their topics. Either way, they will thank you.

PULLING YOUR TEAM OUT OF THE MUD

No doubt you've dedicated yourself to constantly refining your time management skills, blocking distractions, trimming task lists, and otherwise doing what it takes to maximize your work team's productivity.

Among other things, this requires you to cautiously consider each decision before you make it. But tread carefully here. If taken too far, trying to review or prepare for every possible contingency can result in the paralysis of analysis, what I think of as "vapor lock of the brain." Rather than waste your time with indecision, as long as you have enough information and other resources necessary to take action, then "just do it." Nike's famous ad slogan hits this one right on the head. Motion in any direction shatters the ice of indecision.

If you or your team members ever suffer from analysis paralysis—or find yourselves dragging your heels due to uncertainty—put these seven tips into play:

1. *Reject perfectionism.* Everything has some level of downside risk; even "sure things" can blow up in your face. Let's face it: no matter how much time and effort you've spent preparing, you'll probably hit unexpected snags. So stop hesitating and move forward. Prod your team members into action if you must.

2. *Accept the possibility of failure.* Naturally, you want to do your best for yourself and your team, but inevitably a certain percentage of your decisions will prove incorrect. Recognize this fact and stop huddling in place; instead, choose a direction and get moving. If you've picked the wrong way, so be it. You'll soon know and can adjust your course. If you at least learn something worthwhile, then you can't consider any misstep a complete failure.

3. *The simplest solution is probably the best.* Often, the path of least resistance represents the best possible choice. So once you've examined it from all angles and can see no obvious surprises, flaws, or pitfalls, then go for it.

4. *Follow your core values.* If a potential decision conflicts with the things you or your organization believe in most, dismiss it from consideration. Stand secure in the knowledge that your core values will guide the way, whether they revolve around a deity, an absolute belief in people and what they can accomplish, personal and intellectual honesty, or all of the above. This alone will clear the field of many candidates.

5. *Focus on getting started.* Knowing where you want to go and the basic route you need to take represents half the battle. You don't have to sharply define every step before beginning. Handle the fine details on the fly.

6. *Establish milestones and a drop-dead deadline.* Know when you absolutely have to have a task done. Break it into easy pieces that allow you more than enough time to complete it before the final deadline arrives. Hand out the pieces to those who can accomplish them best. This will motivate you to stop wasting time and get started. Nothing beats writer's block, for example, like knowing you face a specific date to turn in a piece, no matter how uncertain you feel about it.

7. *Listen to both head and heart.* Sometimes a certain course of action makes absolute sense from an intellectual perspective, but still seems wrong. If so, your subconscious mind has probably noticed something your conscious mind hasn't. So use both your IQ and your emotional intelligence (EQ) when making

decisions. Don't go overboard here; instinct can lead you astray in some cases. But do consider both sides of the IQ/EQ equation, and make your decision based on which side weighs the heaviest. Again, you may still be wrong, but you need to make a decision and move on.

It's impossible *not* to make a decision. Putting a decision off is itself a decision. If you drag your heels, events will make your decision for you if another person doesn't. You're no puppet, so don't sit there in vapor lock and allow others to pull your strings to determine your team's fate. Shape it yourself with your own timely decisions.

THINKING. TRY A LITTLE.

If you want your employees to be strategic enablers of business, you have to give them time to be strategic. If they're always running around from meeting to meeting, interrupting each other, and returning to an overflowing in-box, they won't have time to focus on high-value tasks. Workers need periods of time when they can think without other people interrupting. They must balance the need to be available with the need to concentrate. It's a delicate balance, but one you can help them achieve. Have them consider the strategies outlined in this part of the chapter and help them implement them if necessary.

You Want It WHEN?

Workplace productivity springs primarily from one's skill at time management, which actually boils down to self-management, since everyone gets the same amount of time. You can't be so good at time management that you create a thirty-hour day for yourself.

Therefore, when setting your schedule, your ability to estimate a task's duration becomes crucial. Estimates come most easily for common tasks or those with familiar elements. Experience tells you what to expect and how much time to allow for them.

The real issue comes when you encounter a completely unfamiliar task. How do you determine the amount of time something new will take you without over- or undershooting it significantly?

Measure Twice, Cut Once

Don't "guesstimate" when calculating the duration of a new task. Instead, research it while keeping the following factors in mind:

- *Watch out for the Planning Fallacy.* According to psychologists Daniel Kahneman and Amos Tversky,[17] most of us underestimate how long we'll take to complete our tasks, even when we've run late on similar tasks before. This tendency stems mostly from wishful thinking and optimism, though it often arises when our superiors push us for an estimate based on everything going perfectly. This rarely occurs, so be realistic. Don't tell your boss it will take you a week to write a report because you assume that absolutely nothing will keep you from completing ten pages a day. Interestingly, the Planning Fallacy applies only to time estimates for one's own tasks; we typically overestimate for other people. Therefore, you may be better off asking someone who knows you well to estimate how long they think you'll take, and then adjust the estimate somewhat.

- *Locate and work with organizational guidelines.* Your company may already have estimates for a given task, based on time-and-motion studies

or long-term experience, so look for basic guidelines. For example, if you have to write a report
explaining sales figures for a particular region by
quarter, your company will almost certainly have
formatting guidelines for reports. It might also
have a stylebook to follow in terms of spelling,
capitalization, grammatical usage, punctuation,
and so on. Learning a new format can add time
to your estimate.

• *Ask team members and others.* Even if no one has
previously documented the task, other people in
your organization, your boss, or a mentor may have
performed it, or at least something like it, before.
So ask around. Remember, you may have to count
the consultation time toward your total time estimate. If you'll be working with others on the task or
delegating it to someone, take the abilities, deficits,
and work styles of those involved into account.
Some teams work together like well-oiled machines;
others have their squeaky wheels. That may require
you to plan for any intra-team issues you can
reasonably expect.

If you still can't pin down how long something will
take, it's better to overestimate than underestimate. Be a
little pessimistic and deliberately build flexibility into your
schedule. If you finish early, you'll have extra time to apply
toward something else.

If experience doesn't offer any guidelines for an unfamiliar task, use the tips I've outlined here to narrow the field.
If they don't help, then make your best guess. You may
be dreadfully wrong; even so, the next time you encounter
that task, you'll have a better basis for your estimate.

DANCES WITH INTERRUPTIONS

According to Julian Treasure, the chairman of The Sound Agency, workers can be up to three times more productive when they work in peaceful environments.[18] Ringing phones, chattering voices, rustling papers, and all the other racket of the standard open-plan office inevitably demand part of their attention—and it takes a lot of subconscious effort to tune out distractions.

As a leader, eliminating workplace distractions is one of your most important tasks—another job for you as the bulldozer. Even small actions like these can help:

- Installing cubicle doors.

- Using noise-canceling headsets.

- Banning loud hallway conversations.

- Allowing your workers to turn off their phone ringers.

- Cutting back on e-mail checking.

As for you, maintaining an "open door" policy—a popular recent business innovation—can be tricky at best. Instead of tolerating random interruptions from your staff to answer questions, schedule and communicate your "interruption availability." Mike Howard, CSO of Microsoft, said,

> As a leader, there's a balance between being available and so available that you can't complete your strategic thinking work. In order to be strategic, I have to find the time to be strategic, and I have to make sure that I'm available for my team to ask questions and clarify direction.
>
> So I've put several mechanisms in place that allow me to stay in touch with all of the people in my organization. I've

started something called [General Manager] GM Hours. Several times a month, anyone in my organization has the ability to sign up for thirty-minute blocks of time to chat with me regarding any subject they want to talk about. We also include my international folks in this program so they can call in from overseas to talk to me. I have received excellent feedback from my team regarding the GM Hours, plus it helps me to keep connected with my entire team regularly.

Another vehicle is that we have quarterly all-hands meetings when I can do updates to everyone globally. I give them a sense of where we are as an organization. It's important to continue to communicate the vision.

Obviously, a "scheduled interruption" technique like Mike Howard's won't work if you have an immediate crisis on your hands. Still, most often it allows both parties to be prepared and available. Alternatively, you can encourage the use of meeting invitations rather than "drop-in" visits.

OBSESSIVE? WHO, ME?

While superior productivity is neither simple nor easily reduced to its component parts, most people agree that productivity requires a focus on priorities—one that excludes the extraneous and strips away anything that doesn't contribute to a specific goal. Some might even call such a tight focus an obsession.

Indeed, people have called me obsessive multiple times. After one such accusation, I explored the concept to determine whether obsession is such a bad thing.

Well, let's see. An obsession is a set of repetitive thoughts at the forefront of your mind, holding your imagination hostage and compelling you to focus your efforts on a single subject. Defined that way, you can indeed consider productive focus an obsession. Perhaps the biggest difference between obsession and focus is that most of us can turn off our productive focus at will, putting it away at the end of the day like any other work tool.

Maybe this is where people confuse the issue. Can you put your work away? Do you work when you ought to rest? Or do you constantly think about what you "should" do when you're not working? Have you tied your sense of self-worth to your to-do list? Do you think of yourself as little more than what you can accomplish?

Perhaps the distinction of control contributes to where the confusion about obsession comes from. Yes, I can put my work away and stop thinking about it. I can certainly go to my son's ballgame and not touch my phone. I do block off six weeks of vacation a year, during which I let my office manager hold down the fort. But when I'm working, I'd agree that my productive focus is obsessive. And when I'm not working, I'm obsessed with not working. I might check into the office, but I control it; I'm checking in by design, not by default. And that's the difference!

Cautious Control

If you ever find yourself wondering if you've fallen prey to a productivity obsession, ask this question: "Do I feel in control of my situation?" If you choose to work seventy hours this week because circumstances demand it, that's one thing. But if you always work seventy-hour weeks and don't really know why, especially if you've compromised your health or relationships in the process, something's wrong. Think long and hard about your work/life balance.

Sustainable Competence

Many psychologists believe obsessions are, by definition, self-destructive. Some buck the trend by insisting that "productive obsessions" can motivate you while allowing you to maintain control of your environment and fate. I see merit in both arguments, but in my experience, you can't sustain even productive obsessions for long. You are not a robot. It's better for you (and your organization) if you burn steadily for a long time rather than flaring briefly and winking out.

So am I obsessed? Yes—about finding a productive focus.

IS SIXTEEN HOURS A DAY ENOUGH, OR AM I SLACKING OFF?

In a public seminar I held recently, one of the participants posed this interesting question: "Laura, how much work is enough? I could work sixteen hours a day, but I'm not sure when to stop! What is a good gauge?"

What a great question! One of the audience members said (half-jokingly), "I stop when I finish my to-do list or can't stay awake any longer." This reminds me of a line by American humorist Robert Orben: "Don't smoke too much, drink too much, eat too much, or work too much. We're all on the road to the grave—but there's no need to be in the passing lane."

Everyone is different, so the answer to the question is "it depends." For example, I work constantly when I'm on the road (over 100,000 miles a year on United Airlines, traveling to speaking engagements). I make the most of my time in airports, on planes, and in hotel rooms so I can spend more uninterrupted time with my family when I'm home and less time working. What's the right mix for you?

Consider this: No matter how productively and efficiently you work, more work always waits for you in the wings. As a Sandra Boynton cartoon featuring a frazzled-looking beaver puts it, "It's just one dam project after another." Some tasks repeat on a predictable cycle, making it difficult to get ahead. Plus, we can always do more to tweak systems and tighten productivity if we have nothing else to work on.

Because there's a never-ending stream of work, you must make a conscious decision not to overwork except when you have to—and then only for short bursts. If you don't, you may end up in a downward spiral of exhaustion and poor health. Even if you do somehow find spare time, you may feel so wound up that you don't know what to do, especially when you start wondering what happened to your family and friends.

To keep that from occurring, set deliberate limits on your work time. No amount of work will make you more productive than a reasonable work/life balance, especially once you hit the point of diminishing returns at about ten to twelve hours a day. As business blogger Slavko Desik points out, "Being taught that more is better, we're jumping to erroneous conclusions way too early, and all of a sudden being more productive has no limits in terms of enough."

Instead of killing yourself with overwork, remind yourself of basic business realities and use techniques that allow you to maintain control no matter what. No one's head will explode if you don't finish a task this second. Furthermore, I doubt doing it tomorrow will get you fired. Few things are so urgent you can't put them off if necessary—especially when you're overextended and exhausted. So be honest, direct, and realistic with yourself.

Juggle Your Expectations and Deadlines

Determine, in advance, the amount of effort it will take to handle a task or project. Then calculate backwards to decide how much you'll need to work on it each day between now and its due date. By doing that, you know you're making the best use of your time each day. Always plan in flexibility in case of emergencies or illness.

Make sure each milestone gets into your time management system and work on your tasks in priority order. That way, you won't suddenly realize you've left all your Priority 1 tasks for the end of the day. Then you have no other choice but to stay until you've finished them, thus creating a self-fulfilling prophecy of overwork.

Strike a Decent Balance

Decide to work no more than a set number of hours each day and stick to your guns. If you had to work a specific number of hours a day, what would have to change for you to achieve it? I know I have to do certain things on my list each day, but other tasks can fall off if I run out of time.

Establish sharp boundaries between work and the rest of your life, too. Once you've left the office, avoid working unless it's an emergency (and define "emergency" very strictly). Take your well-earned breaks, weekends, and vacations as well.

Don't Forget Your Family

A job is only a job. Yes, you want to wow your boss and make a great living, but not at the expense of never seeing your loved ones. If the choice comes down to breaking ties with your family or your workplace, family should win hands down. You can always get another job; you can't get another family without much suffering.

Pay attention to your kids while you still have them (trust me—with my daughter recently graduating from high school, I could feel the time until she left for college ticking in my heart every day). Set a weekly date night with your spouse.

Think of it this way: If you marry your job from the beginning of your career, prepare to be alone when you retire. Decide now whether that will be worth it or not.

Take Care of You

Most people need seven to nine hours of sleep a night, plus everyone needs to eat well and exercise regularly. Schedule your workouts as religiously as you would any of your work tasks, so you can keep your energy up and maintain astonishing productivity. I schedule my run on my calendar five out of seven days a week and stick to it religiously, or I'm a grumpy bear and have horrible energy.

Get a Hobby

Find (or rediscover) something not work-related you love to do. Let it tempt you away from spending too much time at work (even if you love your work, too). If you start feeling antsy about being off work, find a hobby that can fill your time. Do you love to fish, read, write, golf, play cards, ski, or swim? For example, our family has an Aussie puppy I love to play with. As a hobby, I'm working with her on the command "Jump" to prepare for agility trials.

Find something to turn to instead of work, and make that appointment as important as any other on your calendar.

Steady as She Goes

Hard work can be its own reward, but it can also be its own penalty. You only have twenty-four hours in the day. If you work sixteen—as the fellow mentioned earlier seemed willing to do—you won't have much time left for basic functions like cooking and shopping, much less sleep, good health, and enjoyment.

Don't just live to work. Live! While work is crucial, doing nothing but working represents an existence; it's certainly not a life.

THE FINAL WORD

Remember the Biblical story of David and Goliath? It's a classic of its type, right up there with Jack and the Beanstalk. In both cases, a little guy shocks the world by using speed, agility, and audacity to bring down an "unbeatable" giant.

To survive in business these days, companies must become nimble and flexible enough to outmaneuver their competitors, large and small. We've covered the basics of this process in detail throughout this book. But once you've achieved agility and done everything possible to make life easier for your team, you have to show sufficient gumption to maintain your system and tweak it toward perfection. Resting on your laurels is not an option today! So consistently oil your joints, tighten up loose screws, swap out old, worn-out parts, and otherwise retain your preventive maintenance practices, even when everything seems perfect.

Businesses combine some of the features of both living beings and machines; like both, they slow down as they age. We humans settle into our roles, get used to life as it is, and often try (if only subconsciously) to avoid change. In so doing, we may carry otherwise admirable qualities like attention to detail too far. When things like that build up, the organization starts to petrify.

Don't let it happen to you. Open your mind, maintain your health (both mental and physical), limber up, and rededicate yourself to winning the productivity race. Push yourself to do what you must when you must. Avoid the unnecessary and shave wasted time out of your schedule.

Or stay right where you are, complacent and happy, until a young David comes along and pegs you between the eyes with the stone of innovation.

Conclusion

No battle plan survives contact with the enemy.
—*Helmuth von Moltke the Elder,*
nineteenth-century Prussian field marshal

It doesn't matter how good a leader you are if you can't execute your strategy right now, in the moment, in a way that fits conditions as they currently exist—not as they existed five minutes ago, or five months ago, or five years ago. That kind of lag time might have been acceptable once, but the Great Recession and the banking crisis have reset our collective business reality. Today, the only logical strategy is the one that facilitates implementing your task, product, service, or offer in the smoothest, fastest, most cost-efficient way possible.

To reiterate the central thesis and title of this book, execution *is* the strategy that will allow you to remain relevant, innovative, and competitive in the global marketplace of modern business. As a leader, your goal should be to produce results in the form that most pleases your stakeholders and end users, while being consistently achievable by your employees. Admittedly, bringing those two requirements into equilibrium can be challenging.

Not to put too fine a point on it, but only results matter in the end. As a leader, it's your duty and privilege to implement and execute strategies that produce maximum results on every level of the business ladder. If we can't profitably produce, no amount of good intentions will help us.

If you find yourself choking on your competitors' dust, you can't achieve anything worthwhile unless you change your behavior, both as an individual and as an organization. Despite occasional stumbles, wise leaders have begun to realize this truth and act on it.

STRATEGIC PLANNING IN THE NOW

In recent years, companies scrambling to keep up with the frantic pace of our brave new world have changed the way they conduct strategic planning. We've always practiced strategic planning at some level, of course, and we still need it today; but what we meant by the term as few as five years ago barely resembles today's reality. This should come as no surprise in an era when last month's smartphone can't run this month's apps.

Once upon a time, strategic planning was a leisurely process, hidebound and bureaucratic. Some managers still treat it as such; worse, they see strategic planning as something mysteriously created by senior executives and/or outside consultants. They perceive execution as little more than the downstream part of the process. The senior leadership decides what to do, while staff members take the decision and run with it along a very narrow, predetermined path, complete with detailed financials.

We know this process doesn't work well anymore. More often than not, an entire market suddenly shifts, or an employee comes across an opportunity that must be seized in the moment, requiring operational action that in turn alters the strategic direction. So at the end of the year, when (and if) the plan is reviewed, what the executors actually did is often not what the leaders outlined. Companies must adapt on the fly to fit current realities; if they fail to adapt, the company takes a hit. Enough hits, and it'll be down for the count.

STRATEGIC PLANNING BELONGS ON THE FRONT LINE, TOO

Leaders still play a crucial role in strategy, because someone must communicate the goals and priorities to the workers. But today's business world is too unpredictable to straitjacket your front-liners with last year's strategies. Keep the following principles in mind as you proceed with your strategic planning.

Think Around Corners

I could fill another book with things no one thought would ever happen but did anyway—and almost always suddenly. The *Challenger* and *Columbia* space shuttle tragedies. The fall of the Berlin Wall in a matter of days. The collapse of the Soviet Union soon after. CDs and DVDs, which revolutionized data storage and entertainment, and cloud storage soon after. Guns N' Roses even released its album *Chinese Democracy*.

Everything is in a state of flux, more so than at any other time in history. Futurists tell us it will only move faster, such that we can't predict with any clarity what business will be like forty or fifty years from now. Back in the 1950s and 1960s, few people foresaw the modern desktop computer revolution—not even computer experts. Imagine what modern leaders will completely fail to foresee today, simply because we can't imagine how or to what extent things will change.

Clearly, the old-fashioned three-to-five-year strategic

plans don't work anymore. At best, you can only plan a year or so ahead, and even then, you'd better review your strategy quarterly, monthly, weekly, or daily in some cases. Office Depot is an example of a company that caught on to this quickly; in first quarter 2009, the company began reviewing its annual budget monthly, a practice resulting in several profitable mid-course changes thus far.[19] Many companies have followed suit.

Exercise Serious Agility

In today's business environment, you can generate better results if you engage your workers and create an agile corporate culture full of strategic thinkers. The military realized this long ago. The officers don't do the physical work or even decide how to do it; their job is to tell the non-commissioned officers (NCOs) to get it done. The NCOs pass the work down the line; whoever the buck stops with has to figure out how to best accomplish the task. The idea is to just do it and not worry about the planning. Despite common misperceptions, the military has never wanted brainless killers who automatically and thoughtlessly execute their orders. They want well-trained people who can think on their feet and figure out the best way to accomplish a goal.

The same goes for business, especially as we manufacture strategy daily on the front lines. Workers must be empowered to take ownership of their jobs, engage without fear of censure, and act on what they know best without waiting for permission from the chain of command. Many battles have been lost, both in warfare and in business, to slow decision making by home-front leaders. They had no idea what life was like on the front line, or what strategies were required to win the battle where and when it was actually occurring.

Accept Your New Leadership Role

Rather than simply issuing orders and expecting team members to follow them blindly, encourage them to do what they already know they need to do. Accept the fact that, despite your leadership role, they're the ones at the sharp end of the stick. Don't lose sight of the fact that modern leadership is more of a partnership than ever before. Work may not be a democracy, but it's definitely not a dictatorship anymore. Circumstances change too fast.

Be the change leader when you must and the visionary when you can. Give your team all the facts they need to advance, and allow them a free hand to shift course and goals quickly. Let them tell you the best way to achieve your priorities and get out of their way. Maintain the conversation as a positive feedback loop. That way, they know that what works best is constantly added to and strengthens the workflow system.

Engineer Behavioral Change

A big part of your role is getting your team to accept the desirability of change, constantly and consistently. They must be willing to turn on a dime and start doing things differently whenever it's necessary for the team and organization.

The only way you can effectively change strategic execution is by compelling behavioral change among those who work for you. Business as usual has become a dead-end street lined with empty houses. While you can attempt to change strategic execution with the stroke of a pen, what really works is winning the hearts and minds of the people on the front line, so they'll engage sufficiently to make the right changes necessary to keep their jobs—and yours.

Remain Vigilant

Think that's an exaggeration? The global economy has begun to shift in a big way, moving further toward equal distribution between East and West than ever before. As China, India, and other nations make inroads into Western-style standards of living, the Fortune Global 500 has changed significantly. Management consulting firm McKinsey & Company estimates that, by 2025, 45 percent of all Fortune Global 500 companies will be based in emerging nations.[20]

What does that mean for you? It's imperative to keep a constant eye on the horizon in this era of rapid business evolution. You should optimize your business networks to include more emerging marketplace connections, so you can ease into the market change as it occurs. Keep a close eye on both your customer base and your competition, note how their compositions are changing over time, and be prepared to realign your strategy to take advantage of those changes. If you belong to a particularly large organization, consider decentralizing so that at least some of your corporate centers are located in emerging market centers, such as Singapore, Brazil, or China.

You not only have to be prepared for change, but you also have to understand, well in advance, what type of change will most likely occur—so you won't be blindsided by unexpected events.

Couple Wishful Thinking with Positive Action

As hard-nosed as some business people appear to be, we're still susceptible to wishful thinking. Consider it an occupational hazard, especially when the money's rolling in in seemingly endless quantities. But simply wishing for something hard enough won't make it come true, no matter how many celebrities and self-anointed gurus tell you so. So just saying you want to improve your strategic execution is meaningless. You must couple desire with positive action for it to matter.

Now, I'm not saying that being a cheerleader, thinking positive thoughts, and shouting, "Go, Team!" isn't a good start. Indeed, it's absolutely necessary—as long as it motivates you and your team toward something more concrete.

The reality of the last few years has left us shaking off the last remnants of our fantasies as we move into the future . . . if only because many of their proponents have fallen by the wayside. Their fate has made it clear that we have no choice: if we don't face reality as it is, reality will eat us alive.

Charge in the Right Direction

Hard work and high-speed action don't matter one iota when they're pointed in the wrong direction or otherwise poorly executed.

Years ago, a well-meaning California-based environmental action group saved the lives of two seals that had been injured in accidents. After months of surgery, physical therapy, and rehabilitation, the group decided it was best to release them at the Farallon Islands off the coast of California, where there was a large population of seals for them to join. They failed to realize that the waters around the Farallons were frequented by the seals' apex predator, the great white shark; indeed, the "Devil's Teeth," as the islands were nicknamed, were famous for the size of their sharks, some of which rivaled the fictional Jaws of Steven Spielberg's film.

Within minutes of their release, several sharks ate both seals in front of horrified witnesses. One commentator pointed out that the environmental group's actions were the equivalent of lovingly healing a man of a broken leg and then kicking him off a cliff. (If all this seems familiar, it's because the Discovery Channel used a variation of the scenario, starring "Snuffy," for its premiere Shark Week commercial of 2013.)

My point is, reality trumps naive optimism and good intentions every time. The seal team spent a huge amount of money and effort to save the two seals and then completely flubbed the final execution (an especially apt word here).

If you're enthusiastic about your business outlook and spend many hours planning how you're going to achieve your goals, that's great—as long as you combine all that with actual action designed to put your team, department, or organization at the front of the pack, pointed in the proper direction. Business is no longer just dog-eat-dog; it's more shark-eat-shark. You have no choice but to combine optimism with cautious, properly oriented implementation designed to meet change head-on. Otherwise, you may end up as the next Snuffy the Seal.

Realize That Execution IS the Strategy

Today's leaders cannot effectively dictate how to execute strategic priorities anymore; only those who execute can, because everything changes so rapidly. That said, as a leader, you're still responsible for clarifying goals and creating and organizing the strategy, so people know what they're shooting for and have some general way to get there.

Further, you can't accept that a goal has been set until the execution team has adopted it. Never blame your people for failure of strategic execution. If you haven't clarified your objectives well enough that they can name them at the drop of a hat, how can they know what they need to do in order to achieve maximum results? If they're not sure what they're doing, they'll just go through the motions, stay busy, and keep their heads down.

So step in to show them point by point what they must

accomplish and why it matters—and then take steps to reduce the whirlwind of daily work so they have time to execute the bigger goals. Make them accountable for their results, employing accurate means of measuring performance. Offer the right rewards—and, most of all, allow them to adopt flexible operational plans to fit the current reality. Do all this, and they'll achieve wonders for you.

SHIFT YOUR MENTAL MODEL

Strategy is no longer chiseled in stone; it has become as flexible and changeable as life itself. We still need leaders to articulate the mission, vision, goals, and strategy, while the team defines the tactics, which shapes the strategy, as leaders make the course corrections, in a continuous cycle.

Most important, leaders hold us to the core values that define our organizations. Many business leaders of our era have forgotten this. If we fall prey to corruption, self-centeredness, and poor management, we pave the highway straight down. If we keep twisting our core values so far out of alignment that the public no longer trusts us, we're sunk. If we're so busy fighting our own systems that we accomplish nothing of value, we're doomed.

In today's business world, execution itself is the only strategy that matters. A decent strategy, brilliantly executed, will trump a brilliant strategy, poorly executed. As leaders and followers form tighter partnerships, the companies with the stellar strategies that follow the principles of the L-E-A-D Formula will maintain the conditions necessary to hurtle forward. Don't lose sight of what truly matters in the day-to-day battles. Execution truly is the strategy that will propel your organization to success.

▶▶   Go to **www.ExecutionIsTheStrategy.com** to receive complimentary bonus material, videos, tip sheets, and book club materials.   ◀◀

Notes

1. David Z. Hambrick and Elizabeth J. Meinz, "Sorry Strivers, Talent Matters," *New York Times*, November 19, 2011, http://www.nytimes.com/2011/11/20/opinion/sunday/sorry-strivers-talent-matters.html#p5.

2. Geoff Colvin, *Talent Is Overrated: What Really Separates World-Class Performers from Everybody Else* (New York: Portfolio, 2010).

3. K. Anders Ericsson, *The Road to Excellence: The Acquisition of Expert Performance in the Arts and Sciences, Sports, and Games* (New York: Lawrence Erlbaum Associates, 1996). See also Malcolm Gladwell, *Outliers: The Story of Success* (New York: Little, Brown, and Company, 2008).

4. Laura Stack, *SuperCompetent: The Six Keys to Perform at Your Productive Best* (New York: Wiley and Sons, 2010).

5. "Many Managers Don't Encourage Employee Risk-Taking," press release, BlessingWhite Consulting, May 22, 2007, http://www.blessingwhite.com/docDescription.asp?id=179&pid=6&sid=1.

6. *2012 Global Workforce Study: Engagement at Risk: Driving Strong Performance in a Volatile Global Environ-*

ment, Towers Watson Consulting, July 2012, http://www
.towerswatson.com/Insights/IC-Types/Survey-Research-
Results/2012/07/2012-Towers-Watson-Global-Workforce
-Study.

7. *Employee Engagement: What's Your Engagement Ratio?*,
Gallup Consulting, 2010, http://www.gallup.com/strategic
consulting/121535/Employee-Engagement-Overview
-Brochure.aspx.

8. *Engaged Employees Drive the Bottom Line*, Towers
Perrin–ISR, 2003, http://www.twrcc.co.za/Engaged%20
employees%20drive%20the%20bottom%20line.pdf.

9. John Gibbons, *Employee Engagement: A Review of Current
Research and Its Implications*, Conference Board of Canada,
November 2006, http://www.conferenceboard.ca/e-library/
abstract.aspx?did=1831.

10. James K. Harter, Frank L. Schmidt, Sangeeta Agrawal,
and Stephanie K. Plowman, *The Relationship Between
Engagement at Work and Organizational Outcomes*, Gallup
Consulting, February 2013, http://www.gallup.com/strategic
consulting/126806/Q12-Meta-Analysis.aspx.

11. *2012 Global Workforce Study: Engagement at Risk:
Driving Strong Performance in a Volatile Global Environ-
ment*, Towers Watson Consulting, July 2012, http://www
.towerswatson.com/Insights/IC-Types/Survey-Research-
Results/2012/07/2012-Towers-Watson-Global-Workforce
-Study.

12. *Employee Engagement Research Update, January 2013*,
BlessingWhite Consulting, http://www.blessingwhite.com/
content/reports/BlessingWhite_Employee_Engagement_
Research_Report_2013.pdf.

13. Thomas J. Peters and Robert H. Waterman, *In Search of
Excellence* (New York: HarperCollins, 2004).

14. Laura Stack, *What to Do When There's Too Much to Do:
Reduce Tasks, Increase Results, and Save 90 Minutes a Day*
(San Francisco: Berrett-Koehler Publishers, 2012).

15. Jonathan Bernstein, "Know Thyself: The Role of the Vulnerability Audit," *Arizona Attorney* 36, no. 25 (January 2000).

16. Albert H. Huang, Shin-Yuan Hung, and David C. Yen, "An Exploratory Investigation of Two Internet-Based Communication Modes," *Computer Standards & Interfaces* 29, no. 2 (2007): 238–243.

17. Daniel Kahneman and Amos Tversky, "Intuitive Prediction: Biases and Corrective Procedures," *TIMS Studies in Management Science* 12 (1979): 313–327.

18. "Julian Treasure: The 4 Ways Sounds Affect Us," TED Talk, 2009, http://www.ted.com/talks/julian_treasure_the_4_ways_sound_affects_us.html.

19. Joann S. Lublin and Dana Mattioli, "Strategic Plans Lose Favor: Slump Showed Bosses Value of Flexibility, Quick Decisions," *Wall Street Journal Online*, January 25, 2010, http://online.wsj.com/article/SB10001424052748703822404575019283591121478.html?mod=WSJ_mgmt_MiddleSecond Highlights#articleTabs%3Darticle.

20. Richard Dobbs, Jaana Remes, Sven Smit, James Manyika, Jonathan Woetzel, and Yaw Agyenim-Boateng, *Urban World: The Shifting Global Business Landscape*, McKinsey Global Institute Report, October 2013, http://www.mckinsey.com/Insights/Urbanization/Urban_world_The_shifting_global_business_landscape?cid=other-eml-alt-mgi-mck-oth-1310.

Acknowledgments

After writing six books, it's hard not to be redundant in my acknowledgments—but I'm always glad to write them.

First, I thank God for His continued blessings in my life. I can do all things through Christ, who strengthens me. To God be the glory!

I am so grateful for the love and support of my husband, John. He is the bedrock of my life and my best friend. Thank you for your forbearance in the face of my hectic travel schedule and for "holding down the fort."

My three children—Meagan (eighteen), Johnny (fourteen), and James (twelve)—give me so much joy, and I am so proud of all of you! Thank you for being so understanding of my crazy entrepreneurial lifestyle and pretending that you enjoy it when I'm on the road, so we can get those free trips.

People always ask me how I stay so organized given my hectic schedule. The answer is my office manager, Becca Fletcher, who organizes the organizer. She is the grease that keeps the machine running smoothly in my life, and I simply wouldn't be able to function without her. Everyone needs a Becca!

My gratitude goes to my mother-in-law, Eileen Stack, who supports our family with her time in myriad ways.

A big thank-you to my proofreader, Floyd Largent, for his eagle eyes and creative ideas, as well as the many independent reviewers and friends, too numerous to list, who helped make this book better!

I appreciate my editor at Berrett-Koehler, Neal Maillet, for his continued enthusiastic support of my work.

My mentor of more than ten years, Dianna Booher, has unfailingly given her time, encouragement, and experience to help me succeed. Thank you for being the one I think of first when I'm muddling over a new challenge.

I appreciate my professional speaker colleagues, fellow members of the National Speakers Association, who are like an extended family. I travel more than 100,000 miles a year, so this business can get lonely. Our friendships make life fun and interesting.

Special thanks go out to the busy professionals who shared their time, enthusiasm, and viewpoints during our one-on-one interviews on employee productivity and strategic execution. Those quoted in this book include, in alphabetical order:

- John Alberto, Senior Vice President of Human Resources at Combe, Inc.

- Carlos Amesquita, Director of North America Global Business Services at Procter & Gamble

- Roger Blythe, Vice President of Business Analysis at Chick-fil-A, Inc.

- Steven Gangwish, Vice President of CSS Farms

- Debbie Gross, Chief Executive Assistant, Office of the Chairman and Chief Executive Officer at Cisco Systems

- Mike Howard, Chief Security Officer for Microsoft

- Stacy Tetschner, Chief Executive Officer of the National Speakers Association (NSA)

- Janie Wade, Senior Vice President of Strategic Financial Planning and Analysis at Baylor Health Care System

Finally, I especially thank my clients, my audiences, and my readers. After more than twenty years in business, your enthusiasm for my work keeps me curious about the world of productivity.

Index

About the Author

Jason Schoshke

Laura Stack, MBA, CSP, is America's Premier Expert in Productivity™. For more than twenty years, her seminars and speeches have helped professionals, leaders, and teams accelerate individual and team performance, execute efficiently, and improve output in the workplace. Laura uses both high energy and high content to educate, entertain, and motivate audiences to produce greater results at work. Her company, The Productivity Pro, Inc., provides productivity training to successful companies around the globe to help attendees achieve Maximum Results in Minimum Time®. Laura was the 2011–2012 president of the National Speakers Association (NSA) and is the recipient of the Certified Speaking Professional (CSP) designation, NSA's highest earned designation.

Laura is the best-selling author of six productivity books published by Random House, Wiley, and Berrett-Koehler. Her books have been published in more than twenty countries and translated into many foreign languages, including Japanese, Spanish, Korean, Chinese, Taiwanese, Italian, and Romanian. Laura is a columnist for *Success* magazine, and her popular weekly electronic productivity newsletter has subscribers in thirty-eight countries.

Laura has been featured nationally on the CBS *Early Show*, CNN, NPR, and Bloomberg, and in the *New York Times*, *USA Today*, the *Wall Street Journal*, *Entrepreneur*, and *Forbes* magazine. Laura has been a spokesperson for Microsoft, 3M, Skillsoft, Office Depot, Day-Timer, and Xerox. Her client list includes top Fortune 500 companies, including Starbucks, Wal-Mart, Aramark, Bank of America, GM, Wells Fargo, and Time Warner, plus government agencies such as the Internal Revenue Service, the United States Air Force Academy, the Census Bureau, the U.S. Senate, and the Department of Defense.

Laura lives with her husband and three children in Denver, Colorado.

Educational Resources from Laura Stack and The Productivity Pro®, Inc.

BOOKS

What to Do When There's Too Much to Do: Reduce Tasks, Increase Results, and Save 90 Minutes a Day (Berrett-Koehler, 2012)

SuperCompetent: The Six Keys to Perform at Your Productive Best (Wiley, 2010)

The Exhaustion Cure: Up Your Energy from Low to Go in 21 Days (Broadway Books, 2008)

Find More Time: How to Get Things Done at Home, Organize Your Life, and Feel Great About It (Broadway Books, 2006)

Leave the Office Earlier: How to Do More in Less Time and Feel Great About It (Broadway Books, 2004)

ONLINE RESOURCES

Get an eBook of screenshots of amazing Microsoft Outlook Task Tricks: TheProductivityPro.com/Laura

Subscribe to the free weekly Productivity Minute video series, delivered via e-mail: TheProductivityMinute.com

Download the Laura Stack app and receive a free eBook and new productivity content weekly! TheProductivityPro.com/app

Laura's YouTube channel: youtube.com/theproductivitypro

Link with me: linkedin.com/in/laurastack

Follow me: twitter.com/laurastack

Become a Fan of The Productivity Pro®:
facebook.com/productivitypro

Sign up for my free weekly productivity newsletter, The Productivity Pro®: TheProductivityPro.com/subscribe

Laura's blog: TheProductivityPro.com/blog

More than 150 free articles for download and reprinting for your company website, newsletter, or blog: TheProductivityPro.com/articles

Twelve hours of Microsoft Outlook online video training with workbooks: TheProductivityPro.com/Outlook

Free downloadable worksheets, checklists, and resources: TheProductivityPro.com/free

Take the quizzes *free* from Laura's books: TheProductivityPro.com/quizzes

Get a *free* tip of the day via e-mail: TheProductivityPro.com/tip-of-the-day

Resources for purchase (books, CDs, DVDs, self-study audio, video training, MP3s, etc.): TheProductivityPro.com/products-page

INFORMATION

To inquire about having Laura Stack speak at your next meeting, contact:

The Productivity Pro, Inc.

Phone: 303-471-7401

John@TheProductivityPro.com

CONNECT WITH LAURA

Web:
TheProductivityPro.com
Blog:
TheProductivityPro.com/blog
Twitter: @laurastack

Facebook: ProductivityPro
LinkedIn: LauraStack
YouTube: theproductivitypro
Google Plus:
gplus.to/laurastack

Also by Laura Stack

What to Do When There's Too Much to Do

Reduce Tasks, Increase Results, and Save 90 Minutes a Day

Are you tired of constantly being pushed to do more with less? You're in luck. Laura Stack knows your to-do list is already packed to capacity, so she shows you how to accomplish more by doing less. Yes, you read that right. Stack's innovative time-management system lets you work less and achieve more.

Following Stack's step-by-step Productivity Workflow Formula, you'll organize your life around the tasks that really matter and—this is crucial—let go of those that don't. Dozens of practical strategies will help you reduce your commitments, distractions, interruptions, and inefficiencies. You'll shrink your to-do list and save time—around ninety minutes a day—while skyrocketing your results and maintaining your sanity.

Paperback, 192 pages, ISBN 978-1-60994-539-8
PDF ebook, ISBN 978-1-60994-540-4

BK® Berrett–Koehler Publishers, Inc.
San Francisco, *www.bkconnection.com*   **800.929.2929**

✦ Berrett–Koehler
BK̅ Publishers

Berrett-Koehler is an independent publisher dedicated to an ambitious mission: *Creating a World That Works for All*.

We believe that to truly create a better world, action is needed at all levels—individual, organizational, and societal. At the individual level, our publications help people align their lives with their values and with their aspirations for a better world. At the organizational level, our publications promote progressive leadership and management practices, socially responsible approaches to business, and humane and effective organizations. At the societal level, our publications advance social and economic justice, shared prosperity, sustainability, and new solutions to national and global issues.

A major theme of our publications is "Opening Up New Space." Berrett-Koehler titles challenge conventional thinking, introduce new ideas, and foster positive change. Their common quest is changing the underlying beliefs, mindsets, institutions, and structures that keep generating the same cycles of problems, no matter who our leaders are or what improvement programs we adopt.

We strive to practice what we preach—to operate our publishing company in line with the ideas in our books. At the core of our approach is stewardship, which we define as a deep sense of responsibility to administer the company for the benefit of all of our "stakeholder" groups: authors, customers, employees, investors, service providers, and the communities and environment around us.

We are grateful to the thousands of readers, authors, and other friends of the company who consider themselves to be part of the "BK Community." We hope that you, too, will join us in our mission.

A BK Business Book

This book is part of our BK Business series. BK Business titles pioneer new and progressive leadership and management practices in all types of public, private, and nonprofit organizations. They promote socially responsible approaches to business, innovative organizational change methods, and more humane and effective organizations.

Berrett–Koehler
Publishers

A community dedicated to creating
a world that works for all

Dear Reader,

Thank you for picking up this book and joining our worldwide community of Berrett-Koehler readers. We share ideas that bring positive change into people's lives, organizations, and society.

To welcome you, we'd like to offer you a free e-book. You can pick from among twelve of our bestselling books by entering the promotional code **BKP92E** here: http://www.bkconnection.com/welcome.

When you claim your free e-book, we'll also send you a copy of our e-newsletter, the *BK Communiqué*. Although you're free to unsubscribe, there are many benefits to sticking around. In every issue of our newsletter you'll find

- A free e-book
- Tips from famous authors
- Discounts on spotlight titles
- Hilarious insider publishing news
- A chance to win a prize for answering a riddle

Best of all, our readers tell us, "Your newsletter is the only one I actually read." So claim your gift today, and please stay in touch!

Sincerely,

Charlotte Ashlock
Steward of the BK Website

Questions? Comments? Contact me at bkcommunity@bkpub.com.

Certified

Corporation
bcorporation.net